Living Religions

Christianity

Lynne Gibson

Heinemann
LIBRARY

H www.heinemann.co.uk/library
Visit our website to find out more information about **Heinemann Library** books.

To order:
☎ Phone 44 (0) 1865 888066
🗎 Send a fax to 44 (0) 1865 314091
🖥 Visit the Heinemann Bookshop at www.heinemann.co.uk/library to browse our catalogue and order online.

Heinemann Library
Halley Court, Jordan Hill, Oxford, OX2 8EJ
Part of Harcourt Limited

Heinemann is the registered trademark of Harcourt Education Limited

Text © Lynne Gibson, 2002

First published in 2002

ISBN 0 431 14986 0 (hardback)
06 05 04 03 02
10 9 8 7 6 5 4 3 2 1

ISBN 0 431 14993 3 (paperback)
07 06 05 04 03
10 9 8 7 6 5 4 3 2 1

British Library Cataloguing in Publication Data
A catalogue record for this book is available from the British Library

Typeset by Artistix, Thame, Oxon
Printed and bound in Spain by Edelvive

Acknowledgements
The publishers would like to thank the following for permission to use photographs:

AKG London/Erich Lessing, p. 14; Andes Press Agency/Carlos Reyes-Manzo, pp. 10, 11, 18, 24, 25, 26 (right), 30, 34, 36, 44, 46, 51 and 55; The Art Archive/Galleria degli Uffizi/Dagli Orti, p. 33; Associated Press/Alastair Grant, pp. 52 and 58 (top); Associated Press/Paras Shah, p. 58 (bottom); Circa Photo Library, pp. 4 (left) and 12; Circa Photo Library/John Fryer, p. 32; James Davies Travel Photography, p. 39; Mary Evans Picture Library, pp. 3, 20 and 21; Robert Harding Picture Library, p. 4 (left); Robert Harding Picture Library/Pearl Bucknall, p. 47; Robert Harding Picture Library/Jeff Greenberg, p. 54; Robert Harding Picture Library/David Martyn Hughes, p. 26 (left); Robert Harding Picture Library/ASAP/Garo Nalbandian, p. 38; Robert Harding Picture Library/Geoff Renner, p. 40; Robert Harding Picture Library/E Simanor, p. 40; Impact/John Arthur, p. 35; Panos Pictures/Paul Smith, p. 42; Science Photo Library/Neil Bromhall, p. 56.

The publishers have made every effort to contact copyright holders. However, if any material has been incorrectly acknowledged, the publishers would be pleased to correct this at the earliest opportunity.

Tel: 01865 888058 www.heinemann.co.uk

Contents

An introduction to Christianity

In this section you will:

- find out how Christianity began and developed
- discover how Christianity spread throughout the Roman Empire
- read about and reflect upon how a modern Christian became a martyr.

The word Christos, written in ancient Greek

What is Christianity?

Christianity is one of the major world religions. It has more followers than any other religious tradition. About a third of the world's population, approximately two billion people, are thought to be **Christian**. There are many different kinds of Christians and Christian communities can be found all over the world.

How did Christianity begin and develop?

Map showing the location of Palestine, now known as Israel

Christianity began in Palestine, a country we now call Israel, two thousand years ago. Jesus and his disciples were Jewish. The Christian religion is based on the life and teachings of Jesus. Christianity was the name given to the new religion which was started by Jesus' **disciples** and followers after his death.

The name of the religion comes from the Greek word Christos which means 'the Anointed One'. This was a very special and important title. It referred to someone who was believed to be a saviour sent by God to bring goodness and peace to the Earth. The **Hebrew** word **Messiah** has the same meaning. Jesus' followers began to refer to him as the **Christ** when they believed he had risen from the dead. Their belief in the **resurrection** made them think that Jesus was a saviour sent by God. They became known as Christians, because they were followers of the Christ, the 'Anointed One'.

Christianity has developed in stages. The early Christians were very keen to spread the 'good news' about Jesus. They referred to Jesus as 'good news' because they believed that he was a saviour sent by God. The **apostles**, in particular, travelled throughout the ancient world telling people about Jesus. The early Christians were unpopular with the Romans who ruled large parts of the world at that time. They were persecuted throughout the Roman Empire and sometimes killed for their beliefs. These people were known as **martyrs**.

The first Christian martyr was Stephen who was stoned to death in Jerusalem by an angry crowd. It is estimated that about 40 million Christians in 220 countries have been killed for their faith over the last 2,000 years. At least 100,000 Christians died for their beliefs during the nineteenth and twentieth centuries.

About 300 years after the death of Jesus, the attitude of the Romans towards Christianity began to change. Constantine, a Roman Emperor became a Christian himself. He is said to have seen a large **cross**, the symbol of Christianity, in the sky before he went into battle with his main rival. Constantine won the battle and believed that the God of the Christians had helped him so he converted to Christianity. In 313 CE Constantine passed the Edict of Milan.

This was a law which stated that Christians should be able to follow their religion without being harmed. Very soon after, instead of being persecuted, Christians were given special privileges. Eventually Christianity became the official state religion and spread to the furthest parts of the Roman Empire .

The stoning of Stephen

'They kept on stoning Stephen as he called out to the Lord, "Lord Jesus, receive my spirit!" He knelt down and cried out in a loud voice, "Lord! Do not remember this sin against them!" He said this and died…'

Acts 7: 59–60

A modern martyr

Maximilian Kolbe was a Polish Roman Catholic **priest**. He was arrested by the Nazis during the Second World War and sent to the Auschwitz concentration camp.

Several prisoners who had attempted to escape from Auschwitz were sentenced to death by starvation. Maximilian voluntarily changed places with one of them, a married man with children. Maximilian was locked in a cell without food for two weeks, and was eventually given a fatal dose of poison on 14 August 1941. Maximilian was officially declared a **saint** of the Roman Catholic Church on 14 August 1982. Francis Gajowinczek, the person whom Father Kolbe saved, attended the ceremony.

'… My commandment is this: love one another, just as I love you. The greatest love a person can have for his friends is to give his life for them…'

John 15: 12–13

A Constantinus in Anglia natus ibiq, Imperator creatus, uisa Cruce, de cœlo audit In hoc Signo Vinces. et Maxentio superato Romam liberat:
B Idem a Siluestro PP. baptizatur, et a Lepra Sanatur. tum ecclesiā templis immunitatibus, et muneribus maximis ornat.

An artist's impression of Constantine at Milvian bridge before he went into battle

Divisions and denominations

In this section you will:
- find out how Christianity split into two centres of power
- learn about different Christian denominations throughout the world and how these are divided.

As Christianity developed, two main centres of power emerged. One group was the Catholic Church which had its headquarters in Rome. The other was the Orthodox Church which was based in Constantinople, now known as Istanbul. In 1054 CE, the Patriarch, the head of the Orthodox Church, accused the **Pope**, the head of the Roman Catholic Church, of **heresy**, having false beliefs.

This was a very serious charge and resulted in the Christian Church being split into two parts: the Roman Catholic Church which is based in Rome and the Orthodox Church which is based in Istanbul. This event is referred to as the **Great Schism**. The Great Schism meant that there were two Christian **Churches** in the world.

During the sixteenth century the Christian Church split into more groups. There were several reasons for this. One reason was that the Roman Catholic Church had become very powerful and many people thought that it was abusing this power. They said that it had forgotten the real message of Jesus and needed to reform or change its practices. In 1517, Martin Luther, a German Priest, nailed a document of protest on the door of Wittenburg Cathedral. The Roman Catholic Church told him to withdraw his remarks and refused to make any changes in the way it operated. Luther was excommunicated which means that he was banned from the Roman Catholic Church. He and his supporters went on to found the Lutheran Churches. For different reasons, similar things happened all over Europe. These events are known as the **Reformation** and led to the founding of four main **Protestant** (from the word protest) Churches: Lutheran, Reformed, Baptist and Anglican.

St Peter's Basilica, Rome and the headquarters of the Orthodox Church in Istanbul

Over time, other people have also become dissatisfied with the Church they belong to. So they have broken away and gone on to form new Churches. The Methodist, Pentecostalist, Salvation Army and Quaker groups have all been formed in this way.

There are many different Christian groups within the Christian Church. Each separate group is called a **denomination**. There are about 25,000 denominations within Christianity. Christians usually belong to a local church which is part of a bigger denomination or Church.

During the seventeenth, eighteenth and nineteenth centuries Christianity was taken to some of the remotest parts of the world by **missionaries**. They travelled to Africa, the Americas, Australia and India and converted people to Christianity.

People who are interested in becoming Christians can attend a ten week Alpha Course. Alpha is an evangelical course run by some Churches. It consists of a series of talks which explore the Christian faith. Many people have become Christians after attending the Alpha Course.

Christianity continues to grow and develop today, mainly through the activity of evangelical Christians. Evangelical Christians believe that it is very important to share details of their faith with others. They tell people about Jesus in the hope that they will want to become Christians. Evangelical Christians stress the importance of the Bible and the need to make a personal commitment to Jesus. They have been very successful in attracting young people to Christianity in recent years.

Christian denominations today

This diagram shows the numbers of Christians in the world in 2001 CE, divided into the major denominations.

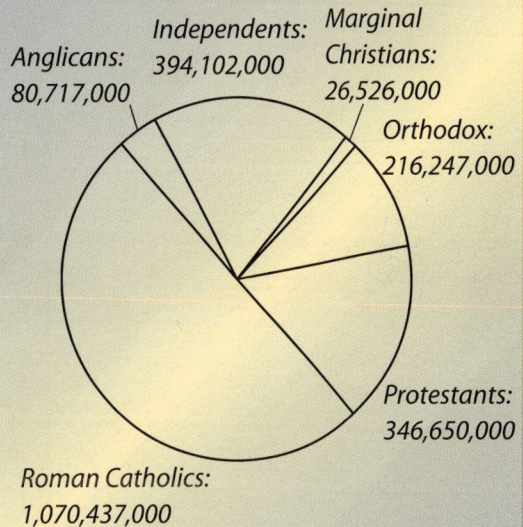

Anglicans: 80,717,000

Independents: 394,102,000

Marginal Christians: 26,526,000

Orthodox: 216,247,000

Protestants: 346,650,000

Roman Catholics: 1,070,437,000

The country with the fastest growing Christian population is China. At one point it was estimated that there were about 10,000 converts a day.

Evidence of Christianity

In this section you will:

- learn how Christianity has influenced the world

- discover how some Christians describe themselves

- have the opportunity to reflect upon what it means to be a Christian and how Christianity might be relevant to your life.

What has Christianity got to do with me?

People who are not religious themselves often think that religion has nothing to do with them. Yet religion can still have an effect our lives even if we are not religious. The diagram below shows some of the ways in which Christianity has influenced the Western world.

Literature

Entertainment

The Calender

Laws

Buildings

Flags

Places

Sport

Christianity has an impact on...

Jewellery

Vocabulary and speech

Business

Name

Charities

The Arts

YMCA/YWCA

Carnivals

Food

Rites of Passage

What is a Christian?

Christians share many common beliefs but they can interpret and practise their faith differently. For example, some Christians have elaborate and energetic forms of worship; others like to keep things simple and prefer to worship in silence. Some Christians choose poverty; others amass great fortunes. Some Christians get involved in political issues in the name of their faith; others believe that religion and politics should be kept separate. Some Christians agree with war in some circumstances; others, called **pacifists**, think that aggression and violence can never be justified. Some Christians accept the use of contraception; others consider it wrong to interfere with nature. Some Christians accept divorce in certain situations; others believe that marriage is forever.

Christians can also have different ideas about what it means to be a Christian. This is what some Christians said when they were asked to describe themselves.

'A Christian is someone who:
…has a personal relationship with God through Jesus
…follows the teachings of Christ
…believes in Jesus Christ
…believes that Jesus is the Son of God
…tries to live their life in the way Jesus wants
…lives according to the teachings of the Christian faith
…has committed themselves to the Christian religion
…belongs to a Church
…has accepted Jesus as their personal saviour
…recognizes that Jesus died to save the world from sin
…has received forgiveness from Jesus
…loves Jesus Christ and their neighbour
…places Jesus at the centre of their lives
…loves and helps their neighbour
…believes in the resurrection of Christ.'

Christianity and education

Traditionally, the **Christian Churches** have set aside the ninth Sunday before **Easter** as Education Sunday. It is a day when Christians remember Jesus as an inspirational teacher. They also pray for everyone involved in the world of education.

Christianity has shaped education in Britain. Early schools were church foundations and a few privileged scholars were taught by **monks**. After the **Reformation**, many great schools and universities were founded. Today, these institutions still have a **chapel** at the heart of the campus, and daily worship in the Christian tradition is an accepted part of the routine.

The industrial revolution saw the need for an educated workforce. Christian groups such as SPCK (the Society for Promoting Christian Knowledge) set up and ran charity schools. Sunday schools also taught people to read and write.

From 1870 CE onwards, other non-Christian organizations established schools. There are still many Church schools in Britain, but most schools are now the responsibility of local education authorities.

In Britain today, Religious Education is a compulsory part of the school curriculum.

Sacred writings – the Bible

In this section you will:

● learn about the Bible and find out what the Bible contains

● look at different Christian attitudes towards the contents of the Bible

● learn about different translations of the Bible

● think about the importance of being able to read the Bible in your own language.

What is the Bible?

The Bible is the **holy** book of **Christians**. The contents of the Bible are sometimes referred to as **scripture** which means sacred writing. The word 'Bible' comes from a Greek word, 'biblia', which means 'books'. The Bible is often treated as a single book but it is in fact a collection of books. These books are thought to have been written by about 40 different people over several centuries.

What does the Bible contain?

The Bible is divided into two parts – the **Old Testament** and the **New Testament**.

The Old Testament is also the Jewish Bible. Jews refer to it as the **Tenakh**. The Old Testament was first written in Hebrew, the language of the Jews. There are several different versions of the Bible. Most English copies of the Old Testament contain 39 books. They tell the story of the Jewish people and contain a mixture of history, laws, songs, prayers, prophecy, poems and psalms. The Roman Catholic **Church** also accepts another collection books, known as the **Apocrypha**, as part of its scriptures.

The Old Testament		The New Testament		The Apocrypha
Genesis	Ecclesiastes	Matthew	1 Timothy	1 Esdras
Exodus	Song of Songs	Mark	2 Timothy	2 Esdras
Leviticus	Isaiah	Luke	Titus	Tobit
Numbers	Jeremiah	John	Philemon	Judith
Deuteronomy	Lamentations	Acts	Hebrews	Esther
Joshua	Ezekiel	Romans	James	The Wisdom of Solomon
Judges	Daniel	1 Corinthians	1 Peter	Sirach (Ecclesiasticus)
Ruth	Hosea	2 Corinthians	2 Peter	Baruch
1 Samuel	Joel	Galatians	1 John	The Letter of Jeremiah
2 Samuel	Amos	Ephesians	2 John	The song of the three
1 Kings	Obadiah	Philippians	3 John	Young Men
2 Kings	Jonah	Colossians	Jude	Susanna
1 Chronicles	Micah	1 Thessalonians	Revelation	Bel and the Dragon
2 Chronicles	Nahum	2 Thessalonians		The prayer of Manasses
Ezra	Habakkuk			1 Maccabees
Nehemiah	Zephaniah			2 Maccabees
Esther	Haggai			
Job	Zechariah			
Psalms	Malachi			
Proverbs				

How the Christian Bible is made up

The Old Testament is important to Christians because they believe it prepares the world for Jesus. Ancient Jewish prophets predicted that one day a **saviour**, the **Messiah**, would be sent by God to bring peace to the earth. Jesus was a Jew and Christians believe that he was the promised Messiah. Jews disagree with this and say that the Messiah is still to come.

The New Testament was first written in Greek and consists of 27 books. Four of these books tell the story of Jesus and his teachings – Matthew, Mark, Luke and John. They are known as the **Gospels**. The word 'gospel' means 'good news', it comes from an Old English word 'godspell' which means 'message from God'. Christians call these books the Gospels because they believe that Jesus was a saviour sent by God which was 'good news' for the world. The Gospels focus on the last few years of Jesus' life. They concentrate in particular on the last week of Jesus' life, known as **Holy Week**. Most of what we know about Jesus is written in the New Testament. The New Testament also tells the story of the beginnings of the Christian Church and contains prophecies about the future.

Christian attitudes towards the Bible

There are three main attitudes towards the Bible. All Christians believe that the Bible is, in some sense, the Word of God. They believe it tells us about God and what God wants for human beings. Some Christians, called fundamentalists, take this literally. They believe that the words in the Bible have come directly from God. They say that the people who wrote the books of the Bible have accurately recorded, word for word, what God has said. Christian fundamentalists believe that everything in the Bible is true because they say God cannot make mistakes.

Other Christians believe that the Bible is accurate or true to God's Word, however, it does not contain the actual words God spoke.

They say that the writers of the Bible have used their own words to express God's thoughts and ideas.

Another opinion is that the Bible has important symbolic meanings. Some Christians believe that the writers of the Bible have used symbolism to explain what they think God meant. They say that the contents of the Bible may not be completely true because human beings are capable of misunderstanding things and making mistakes.

Translations of the Bible

The Bible was originally written in Greek and **Hebrew**. During the fourth century CE, St Jerome translated the Bible into Latin, the common language of the Western Roman Empire. Jerome's translation of the **scriptures** became known as the Vulgate (or 'common version') and was used by the Roman Catholic **Church** for more than 1000 years.

During the fourteenth century CE, an English **priest** called John Wycliffe translated the Bible from Latin into English. Wycliffe wanted everyone to be able to read the Bible for him or herself and not rely on the Church's interpretation. It was very important to him that the Bible and its message got into the language and hearts of the ordinary people. The Church condemned Wycliffe and burned his writings.

At the beginning of the sixteenth century CE, another English priest, called William Tyndale, translated the Bible into English from the original Greek and Hebrew sources. He was convinced that the way to God was through 'His Word' and maintained that even a 'boy that driveth the plough' should have access to the Bible.

How Christians use the Bible

In this section you will:
- find out how Christians use the Bible and what it means to Christians today
- read and reflect upon the story of a woman who went to great lengths to buy a Bible.

How do Christians use the Bible?

Christians regard the Bible as an important source of authority. A source of authority is something or someone which tells you what to do. Christians believe that God 'speaks' to them through the Bible. Christians might read the Bible when they have a problem and need help or when they are upset and need comfort.

The Bible is a source of inspiration, comfort and guidance for most Christians

Some Christians read the Bible every day as an act of private **devotion**. They may follow a set pattern of readings called a **lectionary**. Christians believe that regularly reading the Bible helps them to find out more about their faith. It also helps them to understand how God wants them to live their lives. Sometimes Christians come together in small groups to study the Bible. They discuss what it says and share what they learn with each other. The Bible is also used during public acts of worship. Passages from the Bible are read out during church services.

The Bible is one of the main ways Christians let other people know about their faith. Christians believe that it is part of their religious duty to tell other people about Jesus. One way they do this is by giving away copies of scripture or by putting them in places where people might be likely to read them.

Gideons International is a Christian organization which places Bibles in hotel rooms, prisons and in doctors', dentists' and solicitors' waiting rooms. They also give **New Testaments** to pupils in schools and put copies of the **Psalms**, a collection of religious songs in the **Old Testament**, and the New Testament, in hospital wards. Many people say that they decided to find out more about Christianity and eventually became a Christian after coming across a Bible this way.

The Bible is an all-time bestseller even though copies are often given away free of charge. More copies of the Bible are sold each year than any other book. The Bible is also available in Braille, on cassette, CD-ROM and the Internet. Some parts of the Bible have been translated into more than 2,200 different languages. The United Bible Society is a non-denominational organization which translates, produces and distributes the Christian Scriptures all over the world. Its aim is to provide copies of scripture in languages people can understand and at prices they can afford.

What do Christians say about the Bible?

'Whenever I have a problem or need help I open the Bible at random and read what it says carefully. I don't know how it works but the bit I read always seems to be relevant.'

'I really enjoy studying the Bible. There is always something new to learn.'

'The Bible is the most amazing book, full of wisdom and wonderful stories!'

'I believe that God 'speaks' to us through the Bible and by reading it we can learn what he expects of us.'
'The Bible tells me about Jesus. It makes him real.'

'I believe that by respecting the Bible I am showing respect to God.'

'The Bible is the key to the past, the present and the future.'

'Reading the Bible makes me feel closer to God.'

The story of Mary Jones

Mary Jones was born on 16 December 1784 CE in Wales. She longed to have a Bible of her own, but she could not because her family were too poor. So Mary decided to try to earn enough money to buy a Bible of her own by washing other people's clothes in the river, weeding gardens, knitting socks and looking after children. Eventually, after six years of saving, she had enough money to buy a Bible, but there were none for sale in her village.

In the summer of 1800 CE, Mary walked 25 miles to see if she could buy a Bible from the Reverend Thomas Charles in Bala. He had one copy left but it was already put to one side for someone else. When the Reverend heard Mary's story he made her take the last Bible. He felt that the other person could wait a little longer! Mary's story led to the founding of the British and Foreign Bible Society.

Jesus

In this section you will:

- find out what information Christians have about Jesus
- learn about important events in Jesus' life
- look at some of the ways Jesus has been represented in Christian art
- learn about religious experiences and how they affect people.

Who is Jesus?

Jesus is the most important figure in Christianity. His life, death, **resurrection** and teachings form the basis of the Christian religion and faith. Most of what we know about Jesus is found in the **Gospels**, the first four books of the **New Testament**.

What did Jesus look like?

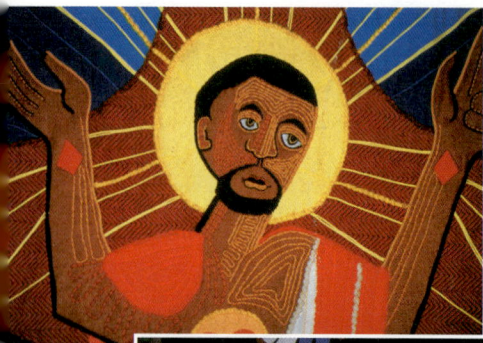

Christians all over the world have produced images of Jesus although no one knows exactly what he looked like

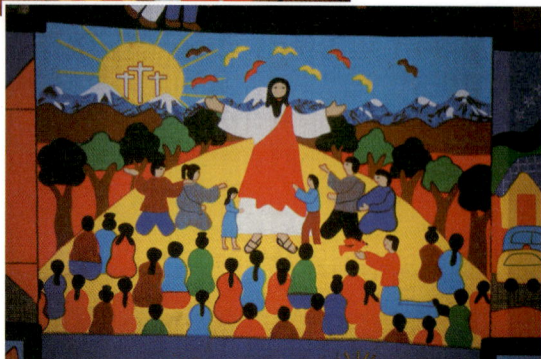

Curriculum Vitae for Jesus

Titles given to Jesus by his followers: Jesus **Christ**, Son of God, The **Messiah**, **Saviour**, Son of Man, Lord.

Titles given to Jesus by his enemies: King of the Jews, Blasphemer, Rebel.

Date of Birth: 6–4 BCE traditionally commemorated on 25 December (Christmas Day).

Place of Birth: Bethlehem, Palestine (now called Israel).

Home Town: Nazareth, Palestine (now called Israel).

Parents: Mary, God and Joseph.

Religion: Jewish.

Occupation: Carpenter and Rabbi (a Jewish teacher).

Hobbies and Interests: Teaching people about God, healing and helping others, storytelling, miracle working, socializing with friends.

Closest Friends: Lazarus, Martha, Mary, Mary Magdalene and the twelve disciples: Simon Peter, John, James, Matthew, Bartholomew, Andrew, Judas Iscariot, Thomas, James, Judas, Simon and Phillip.

Other Associates: The poor, the sick and the outcasts of society.

Significant Moments:

- being taken by Mary and Joseph to Egypt when he was a baby
- being presented in the Temple, the main place of Jewish worship, as a baby
- getting lost on a visit to Jerusalem, the Jewish holy city, with Mary and Joseph and being found three days later in the Temple where he was listening to the Jewish leaders
- being baptized in the River Jordan by his cousin John the Baptist shortly before he began his ministry

- his first miracle: turning water into wine at a wedding in Cana

- his triumphant entry into Jerusalem riding on a donkey (traditionally commemorated on **Palm Sunday**)

- weeping over the state of Jerusalem

- overturning the merchants' tables in the Temple

- sharing a final meal with his disciples (now known as the **Last Supper** where he asked them to eat bread and drink wine in his memory)

- standing trial and being sentenced to death by Pontius Pilate, the Roman Governor

- death by crucifixion

- overcoming death (the Resurrection, traditionally commemorated on **Easter Day**)

- ascending to heaven to be with God (known as the **Ascension**).

Special Achievements:

- surviving forty days and nights in the desert and resisting temptation from the Devil

- healing the sick and crippled

- restoring the sight of the blind

- raising Lazarus from the dead

- feeding 5,000 people with two loaves of bread and five fishes

- walking on water

- calming a storm

- overcoming death (the Resurrection, traditionally commemorated on Easter Day)

- saving the world from sin (**Redemption**)

- repairing the relationship between God and human beings (**Reconciliation**).

Date, time and place of death: In Jerusalem on the Friday before **Pesach** 30–3 CE.

Means of death: Crucified by the Romans at the request of the Jewish religious leaders who accused him of **blasphemy**.

Where do Christians believe Jesus is today?

Christians believe that Jesus is 'alive'. They say that Jesus is in Heaven with God the Father and his spirit, known as the **Holy Spirit**, is active in the world today. Some Christians claim to have met or felt the presence of the 'risen' or resurrected Jesus. Most of these Christians also say that these encounters have changed their lives dramatically. This kind of occurrence is known as a religious experience. Religious experiences can take many forms but they are all events in which people believe that they have in some way come very close to God.

An encounter with the risen Christ

Metropolitan Anthony Bloom, leader of the Russian Orthodox **Church** in Britain, says that he had an encounter with the risen Jesus whilst he was reading the **Gospel** of Mark, in an attempt to prove to himself that Christianity was untrue!

'Before I reached the third chapter, I suddenly became aware that on the other side of my desk there was a presence… the certainty was so strong that it was **Christ** standing there that it has never left me. This was the real turning point. Because Christ was alive and I had been in his presence I could say with certainty that what the Gospel said about the crucifixion of the prophet of Galilee was true, and the centurion was right when he said, "Truly he is the Son of God."'

The early Christian leaders

In this section you will:

- find out about Peter and Paul, two leaders of the early **Christians**
- learn about Paul's four **missionary** journeys during which he founded churches throughout the Roman Empire.

Peter

One of Jesus' disciples, Peter, went on to become the most important leader of the early **Christian Church**. Again, most of what we know about him is found in the **New Testament**.

Jesus changed Peter's name from Simon to Peter.

A early Christian sculpture showing Jesus (centre) with the apostles Peter and Paul

The name Peter comes from the Greek word 'petros', which means rock. Jesus told Peter that he would be the 'rock' upon which he would build his Church.

> And so I tell you Peter: you are a rock, and on this rock foundation I will build my church, and not even death will be able to overcome it.
>
> Matthew 16: 13–20

After Jesus' death, Peter taught and led the early Jewish Christians. He also went on long missionary journeys around Asia. The New Testament contains two letters (**epistles**) he wrote to the Christian Churches there. Peter, like many of the early Christians, was persecuted, imprisoned and eventually died for his beliefs. He was crucified in Rome, probably sometime during 67 CE. Peter chose to be crucified upside down as a sign of respect to Jesus.

Peter is regarded as the first **Pope** of the Roman Catholic Church and is a **saint** of the Christian Church. St Peter's Basilica in Rome was built in honour of him and has a **shrine** containing his remains. Millions of Christians visit it every year. It is the most popular shrine in the Western world. Peter's special status is often symbolized by him being placed next to Jesus in paintings, carvings and sculptures.

Christians are encouraged by Peter's story. This is because he is seen to make many mistakes yet he is still chosen by Jesus to look after and lead his followers. One of the things Peter did was to deny knowing Jesus three times before the crucifixion.

Paul

The New Testament also tells the story of Paul, another very important figure in the development of Christianity. Paul is sometimes referred to as an apostle even though he was not one of the original twelve disciples.

This is because many people think that Paul, more than any other person, was responsible for turning Christianity into a religion.

Paul, originally called Saul, was Jewish and a Roman citizen. He went to Jerusalem to study and became a well-known persecutor of Christians. Paul is said to have been responsible for the death of Stephen, the first Christian martyr.

One day whilst on the road to Damascus, Paul had an experience which was to dramatically change his life.

As Saul was coming near the city of Damascus, suddenly a light from the sky flashed round him. He fell to the ground and heard a voice saying to him, 'Saul, Saul! Why do you persecute me?'

'Who are you, Lord?' he asked.

'I am Jesus, whom you persecute,' the voice said. 'But get up and go into the city where you will be told what to do.'

The men who were travelling with Saul had stopped, not saying a word; they heard the voice but could not see anyone. Saul got up from the ground and opened his eyes, but could not see a thing. So they took him by the hand and led him into Damascus. For three days he was not able to see, and during that time he did not eat or drink anything.

Acts 9: 3–9

Then a Christian called Ananias visited him and cured his blindness.

Paul was convinced that he had encountered the risen Jesus. He stopped persecuting Christians and converted to Christianity. Paul then spent several years in the desert praying and meditating before going on to be the greatest missionary in the history of the Christian Church. Paul believed that the 'good news' about Jesus was for everyone to hear. He travelled around the Roman Empire preaching to Gentiles (non-Jews) as well as Jews and founded many new Christian churches.

Paul wrote epistles (letters) to these new Christian communities offering encouragement and guidance. His epistles are in the New Testament and provide a lot of information about the early Christian Church. No one knows for sure what happened to Paul. Historians think that he was martyred for his beliefs and probably killed by Nero, a Roman Emperor, in 64 CE.

Like Peter, Paul is a saint of the Christian Church. His special status is also often symbolized by him being placed next to Jesus in paintings, carvings and sculptures.

Paul's missionary journeys

Paul made four separate journeys around the Roman Empire, spreading the message of Christianity and founding new **churches** in many places.

The first journey, in about 45 or 46 CE, took Paul from Antioch in Syria to Cyprus, and then on to present-day Turkey. He returned home via the same route.

Paul's second journey lasted four years (48–51 CE). Again, he set off from Antioch, and stopped at all the places where he had established churches on his first journey. He then went on to Greece, staying in Corinth for eighteen months before returning home.

Two years later, Paul set off again. He travelled through present-day Turkey, spending two years in the city of Ephesus before moving on to Greece and then back to Turkey. He returned by ship to Jerusalem.

In Jerusalem, Paul was arrested and spent two years in prison. He appealed to be tried before the Roman Emperor and was taken, under guard, by ship to Rome. He was forced to spend months in Malta when the ship was wrecked in a gale. When he finally reached Rome, he was able to preach for two years whilst awaiting trial.

Leaders of the Christian Church

In this section you will:

- find out how three of the main Christian Churches are organized
- look at the role of the **priest** within the community
- learn about the role of the **Pope** and how Roman Catholics view him.

The **Christian** faith is divided into many different **denominations**. The table below describes how the three main Christian **Churches** are organized.

Today, most Christians belong to one of the three main denominations: Anglican, Orthodox and Roman Catholic. These churches all have a hierarchical structure which means that there are various levels of authority. Another similarity is that they all have a ministry of bishops. Churches which have a ministry of bishops are known as **episcopal** (taken from a Greek word which means bishop).

Name of Church	The Protestant Churches	The Roman Catholic Church	The Orthodox Churches
Divisions within the Church	The Protestant Churches include all the denominations which developed as a result of the **Reformation**. In England, the main denomination is the Church of England (Anglican).	There are no separate branches of the Roman Catholic Church.	The Orthodox Church is made up of fifteen national or regional Churches.
Leaders and followers	Members of the Church of England are known as Anglicans. Their way of understanding and following the Christian faith is one form of Protestantism. Each Protestant denomination has its own organizational structure and some involve the ordinary members of the **congregation** (**laity**) more than others. The Queen is, officially, the head or 'Supreme Governor' of the Church of England. Under the Queen are two Archbishops (senior bishops). Each archbishop is responsible for a particular part of the country. Under the archbishops there are bishops who oversee the running of several churches within a large area called dioceses. Archdeacons rank just below bishops and help them carry out their duties. In each diocese there are priests (vicars) who are responsible for a specific parish or local community within the diocese. Priests are often helped by deacons, people who are training to be priests.	Members of the Roman Catholic Church are known as Roman Catholics. Their way of understanding and following the Christian faith is called Catholicism. The Roman Catholic Church has one leader called the **Pope**. The Pope is elected by cardinals. Under the cardinals there are bishops who oversee the running of several churches within a large area. These areas are called dioceses. In each diocese there are priests who are responsible for a specific parish or local community within the diocese. Priests are often helped by deacons, people who are training to be priests.	Members of an Orthodox Church are known as **Orthodox** Christians. Their way of understanding and following the Christian faith is called Orthodoxy. Each Orthodox Church is independent and has a leader called a Patriarch which means 'great father'. Under each Patriarch there are bishops who oversee the running of several churches within a large area. These areas are called dioceses. In each diocese there are priests who are responsible for a specific parish or local community within the diocese. Priests are often helped by deacons, people who are training to be priests.
Women priests	Several Protestant Churches allow women to become priests. The Church of England has allowed women priests since 1994.	The Roman Catholic Church does not allow women to become priests.	The Orthodox Church does not allow women to become priests.
Religious orders	The three main demoninations each have monks and nuns, groups of men and women who take vows of poverty, chastity and obedience, and dedicate their lives to serving God. Many live a life of service in the community, but some belong to 'enclosed' or 'separate' orders. This means they have very little contact with the community or outside world.		

The role of the priest within the community

Priests often have many roles within the community. One of the main duties of a priest is to look after the spiritual welfare of the people who live in their parish, the geographical area associated with the church. This means that they are responsible for teaching people about God and helping and encouraging them to live their lives according to the teachings of the Christian religion. Christians believe that priests are authorized to forgive people their sins in the name of God. They can lead the community in prayer and worship, celebrate **Holy Communion**, baptize people and prepare them for confirmation and marriage, perform marriage ceremonies and conduct funerals. Christians believe that priests also have an obligation to look after the emotional and physical welfare of the people who live in their parish. This might involve counselling the sick, lonely or depressed and visiting the elderly or people in prison. Other activities of a priest could include running youth groups, visiting schools, meeting with other church leaders, and contributing to the work of the Church in the world. A priest must also find time for personal **prayer** and reflection.

The role of the Pope

Based on the example set by Peter (the **disciple** Jesus chose to lead and look after his followers), Roman Catholics believe that the **Pope** has a unique responsibility for the government (running) of the Roman Catholic **Church** and the welfare (care) of its members. According to Roman Catholic teaching, the Pope has authority from God to forgive sins, set out the beliefs of the Roman Catholic Church and discipline members who go against these beliefs. The Pope is expected to keep the **Christian** faith true to the teachings of Jesus and the traditions of the **apostles**.

According to Roman Catholic teachings, the Pope is infallible. This means that when he speaks *ex cathedra* ('from the chair', in his official capacity as Pope, Jesus' representative on earth) he is never wrong. Roman Catholics believe that God prevents the Pope from making any errors and that his teachings must therefore be followed.

'A day in the life of an Anglican priest'

9.00am–9.30am Morning Prayer service.

9.30am–10.00am Personal prayer and reflection.

10.00am–11.00am Mid-week Holy Communion service.

11.00am–11.30am Coffee with church youth worker.

11.30am–1.00pm Hospital visit.

2.00pm–3.30pm School assembly and meeting with teachers.

4.00pm–5.00pm Bereavement counselling and funeral planning. A home visit to offer comfort to a grieving family and help plan a funeral.

6.30pm–7.30pm **Confirmation** preparation class.

8.00pm–8.30pm Administration, paper work, and preparation for the next day.

8.30pm–9.00pm Read through the agenda for the next Council for Emissions Society meeting.

9.00pm–9.30pm Personal prayer and reflection.

What do Christians believe?

In this section you will:

- study a Christian statement of belief called the Apostles' Creed
- find out what Christians believe to be true about God, Jesus, the world and life after death
- read and reflect upon part of a Christian creed called the Nicene Creed.

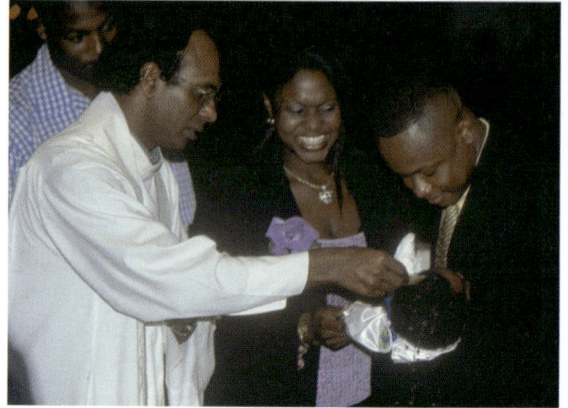

Infant baptism is the ceremony by which babies and children are welcomed into the Christian church

The early **Christians** had many different ideas about their religion, including the identity of Jesus. There were lots of disagreements. Christian leaders thought it was important that everyone knew and agreed upon the basics of the Christian faith. So, during the fourth century CE, two **creeds** (statements of belief) were produced. The word 'creed' comes from the Latin word 'credo' which means 'I believe'. One of these creeds was called the **Apostles'** Creed. It is called the Apostles' Creed because it summarizes the teachings of the apostles, the original twelve **disciples** of Jesus, and sets out the main Christian beliefs.

The Apostles' Creed is an **ecumenical** symbol of the Christian faith. This means that it represents the beliefs of most Christians no matter what denomination they belong to. Anglican and Roman Catholic Churches use the Apostles' Creed regularly during daily prayer and worship. The Apostles' Creed is also a symbol of infant baptism. It describes the faith into which the person being baptized is entering. Sponsors say the Creed during an **infant baptism** ceremony. A sponsor, also known as a godparent, is someone who makes vows on behalf of the person being baptized and promises to help bring them up in the Christian faith.

The Apostles' Creed

I believe in God, the Father almighty,
creator of heaven and earth.
I believe in Jesus **Christ**, God's only Son, our Lord.
He was conceived by the **Holy Spirit**
and born of the **Virgin Mary**.
He suffered under Pontius Pilate,
was crucified, died, and was buried.
He descended to the dead.
On the third day he rose again.
He ascended into heaven,
and is seated at the right hand of the Father.
He will come again to judge the living and the dead.
I believe in the Holy Spirit,
the holy catholic Church,
the communion of saints,
the forgiveness of sins,
the **resurrection** of the body,
and the life everlasting. Amen.

What does the Apostle's Creed reveal about Christian beliefs?

Christians believe that there is one God who has made Himself known to the world in three ways:

Father, Son and Holy Spirit. This does not mean that Christians believe there are three gods. Christians believe that there are three persons in the one God: God the Father, God the Son and God the Holy Spirit. The belief that there are three persons within one God is called the **Trinity**. It is a very important Christian belief. The word 'trinity' comes from the word 'tri-unity' which means three-in-one.

Christians agree that the way the Trinity works is mysterious and difficult to explain. They believe that each person of the Trinity performs a special function: God as the Father created Heaven and Earth, God as the Son is the **saviour** of the world and God as Holy Spirit is an invisible power which guides and inspires human beings.

Christians believe that Jesus is the Son of God, sent to earth by God to save the world from **sin**. They believe that Jesus' death made up or atoned for everything human beings had done wrong since they were first created by God. Jesus redeemed (freed) human beings from sin by his death on the **cross**. This meant that human beings were no longer separated from God by their sins (wrong doings). Christians believe that Jesus made it possible for human beings to have a personal relationship with God.

Christians believe that Jesus was both fully human and **divine**. They believe that God became a man in Jesus. This mystery is known as the **Incarnation**.

Christians believe that Jesus was crucified and died. They believe that he overcame death and rose from the dead three days after he was crucified. This is the central belief of Christianity and known as the Resurrection.

Christians believe that Jesus left the earth forty days after his resurrection. They believe that he ascended (went up) into the presence of God where he occupies a place of honour. The state of being with God after death is known as Heaven.

Christians believe that Jesus will return to Earth one day to judge people and decide who should go to Heaven. This belief is known as the **Second Coming**. It is called the Second Coming because it will be the second time Jesus has come to earth.

Christians believe that faithful Christians, like the early Christian **martyrs** and **saints**, are now in the presence of God.

Christians believe that they are part of a wider Christian community which includes many different Churches.

Christians believe that God forgives the sins of human beings if they repent. This means that they are truly sorry for what they have done wrong. **Forgiveness** and **repentance** are important themes in Christianity.

Christians believe that there is life after death. The idea of **eternal life** is very important to Christians.

The Nicene Creed

The Nicene Creed is a statement of faith used by most Christians. It focuses on the identity of Jesus and the origins and status of the Holy Spirit. This is an extract from the Nicene Creed.

We believe in one God,
    the Father, the Almighty,
    maker of heaven and earth,
    of all that is, seen and unseen.
We believe in one Lord, Jesus Christ,
    the only Son of God,
    eternally begotten of the Father,
    God from God, Light from Light,
    true God from true God,
    begotten, not made,
    of one Being with the Father.
    Through him all things were made.
    For us and for our salvation
        he came down from heaven:
    by the power of the Holy Spirit
        he became incarnate from the Virgin Mary,
        and was made man.

Sources of Christian belief

In this section you will:

- investigate the various sources of Christian belief
- discover how some Christians believe that God has revealed Him or Herself to them and the impact this has had on their lives
- read and reflect upon part of a Christian poem which praises God and all life.

Christians base their beliefs on what they believe to be true about God and His or Her plans for the world. They believe that God has made Him or Herself known to human beings in a variety of ways. The idea of self-disclosure or God making Him or Herself known to human beings is called **revelation**. There are various sources of revelation in Christianity.

Christians believe the Incarnation is one of the main ways God has revealed Him or Herself to human beings. Jesus' life, death and **resurrection** are a source of revelation and inspiration for all Christians. They believe that Jesus taught them a lot about God and how God wants human beings to live, and His or Her plans for them.

Christians believe that the **Holy Spirit** and the Bible are also sources of revelation and inspiration. Some Christians, known as Charismatic Christians, believe that God, the Holy Spirit, moves people to freely express their joy and delight about their faith. This might include clapping, raising their hands in the air or singing and praying in a special language known as tongues.

Christians believe that the Bible tells them a lot about God, life and the way to **salvation**.

Sports professional Jonathan Edwards claims:

'The Bible is God's word to me, to all of us, to what my attitudes, my actions and the way I live my life should be. Its God's primary way of speaking to me. From the Bible I take the basic philosophy of what I try to do – to glorify God through every aspect of my life'.

Another idea is revelation received through personal experience of God. Many Christians claim to have encountered God through dreams and visions. They believe that these experiences have helped them to understand what God is like and how God expects human beings to live.

Julian of Norwich

During the middle ages a woman known only as Julian of Norwich claimed to have had a series of sixteen visions in which God's love was revealed to her. Julian of Norwich was an anchoress. An anchoress was someone who had taken a vow to live in solitary confinement and devote themselves to prayer and meditation.

Julian of Norwich lived in a cell, or small room, adjoining a church

They were usually confined to a cell or small room adjoining a church. Julian is believed to have seen her visions whilst she was very ill and near death. She recovered from her illness and went on to write two books about her experiences called *Revelations of Divine Love*.

Julian surprised people by repeatedly referring to God and Jesus as 'Mother'. This was very unusual as most Christians then thought that God was male and referred to Him as 'Father'. Julian is also remembered for her optimism. Her visions enabled her to claim, 'All shall be well, and all shall be well, and all manner of things shall be well'.

One day Francis came across a leper and despite being repelled by what he saw, Francis jumped down and kissed the leper's hand. The leper kissed him back and Francis felt a great sense of joy. A few moments later, the leper was nowhere to be seen. Francis was convinced that he had been tested by God and passed. Shortly afterwards, he had another experience. Whilst praying in an old dilapidated church in front of a crucifix, he heard Jesus speak to him, 'Francis repair my church'. Francis rebuilt the ancient church and went on to found a religious order, a community of monks who followed very strictly the way of life Jesus demonstrated in the Bible.

St Francis of Assisi

Francis of Assisi was born in Italy during the twelfth century. He claimed to have experienced several personal revelations of God which changed the course of his life.

Francis is the patron saint of ecologists, people who study the relationships between animals and their environment. He is said to have developed extraordinary relationships with animals.

The Canticle of Brother Sun

Francis of Assisi wrote a beautiful poem in which he praised God and everything that God had created: the sun, the moon and stars, wind and water, fire and earth – and life itself. It is known as 'The Canticle of Brother Sun', and here is an extract.

Praised be You, my Lord, with all your creatures, especially Sir Brother Sun,
Who is the day and through whom You give us light…
Praised be You, my Lord, through Sister Moon and the stars…
Praised be You, my Lord, through Brother Wind,
and through the air, cloudy and serene, and every kind of weather…
Praised be You, my Lord, through Sister Water, which is very useful and humble and precious and chaste.
Praised be You, my Lord, through Brother Fire, through whom You light the night…
Praised be You, my Lord, through our Sister Mother Earth,
who sustains and governs us,
and who produces varied fruits with coloured flowers and herbs.

Symbols of the Christian faith

In this section you will:

- learn about some of the main symbols Christians use and find out what they can tell us about Christian beliefs
- discover the significance of these symbols for Christians today
- gain an understanding of the Christian symbol of the fish.

The cross and crucifix

The **cross** is the main symbol of Christianity. The cross can be found in various forms and can have different meanings. For example it can stand for sacrifice, **salvation** and **reconciliation**. But the cross mainly represents the Christian belief in the **resurrection** – the idea that Jesus overcame death and rose from the dead. **Christians** believe that this means there is life after death.

The cross can be used as a sign as well as a symbol. On maps it shows where a church can be found.

The crucifix is a particular kind of cross. It has an image of the crucified Jesus on it. This symbol focuses on the suffering and death of Jesus. It reminds Christians of the sacrifice he made. Christians believe that Jesus died so that human beings could be forgiven their sins and enjoy a new relationship with God.

Bread and wine

The symbols of bread and red wine are used to represent Jesus' body and blood. The **Gospels** that before Jesus died he shared a meal with his **disciples** now known as the **Last Supper**. Here he asked his followers to break and eat bread and drink wine together in memory of him. Eating bread and drinking wine has become an important part of some Christian worship since this time.

Then Jesus took a cup … and said, 'Take this and share it among yourselves …' Then he took a piece of bread … broke it, and gave it to them, saying, 'This is my body which is given for you. Do this in memory of me.'

Luke 22: 17–19

Water

Every living thing needs water to survive and it is often seen as a symbol of life. Some Christians use water as a symbol because they believe that Jesus offered people the opportunity of a new life with God. Water is used in a symbolic way during **baptism**. It represents spiritual cleansing, the idea of washing away sins and starting again.

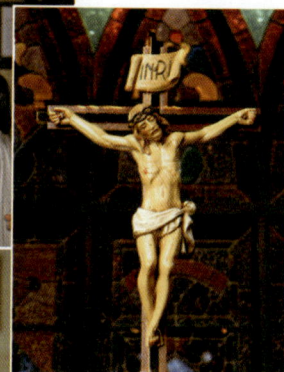

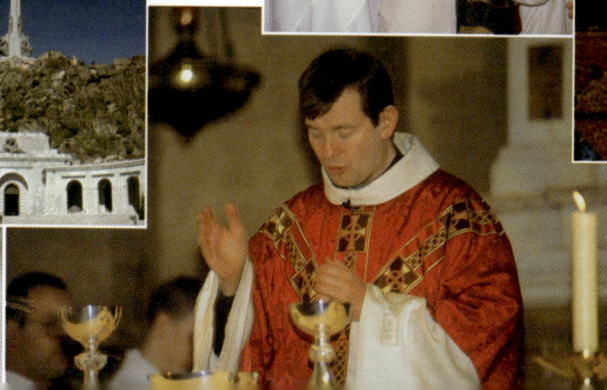

Symbols are important to the Christian faith

Oil

Some Christians use oil as a symbol of healing because, like ointment, it can be rubbed into cuts and burns to make them better. It represents spiritual power. Christians are sometimes **anointed** with **consecrated** oil when they are sick in the hope that God will heal them. They might also have oil put on them during **confirmation** or **chrismation**. This shows that the wounds caused by wrong thoughts or actions are healed. They can put the past behind them and make a fresh start.

In the past important and powerful people like kings were anointed with oil. Oil is seen as a sign of Jesus' kingship: his power and ability to rule over the world. It is still used during some coronation ceremonies.

Some Christian thoughts today

'To me the cross is the most important symbol. It points the way to heaven and reminds me that there is life after death.'

'When I take the bread and wine it reminds me of the sacrifice Jesus made. I feel humble and privileged that God cares so much about us. This act of worship gives me a sense of fellowship and community with other Christians.'

'I was baptized when I was an adult. During the service I was immersed in a pool of water. Before becoming a Christian I had not led a particularly good life. When I came out of the water I felt that everything I had done wrong in the past had been washed away. I knew that God had forgiven me.'

'Fifteen years ago I was very ill and given only six months to live. I was anointed with oil during a healing service. I see oil as a symbol of God's love and His power and ability to help and heal us.'

The symbol of the fish

The fish is one of the oldest **Christian** symbols. The early Christians used the symbol of the fish to communicate safely with each other. It can be found on graves in the Catacombs in Rome, a place where Christians used to meet in secret. Christians also use the symbol of fish today. It has a number of different meanings.

The symbol of the fish reminds Christians of some of the things Jesus is believed to have done. The Gospels say that Jesus called his **apostles** 'fishers of men', and that he fed 5,000 people with just five loaves of bread and two fishes. Another meaning is that the fish represents Christian beliefs about Jesus. This is because the letters in the Greek word for fish, *icthus*, are the first letters in the phrase: *Iesous Christos, Theou Huios, Soter*. These words mean 'Jesus Christ, Son of God, **Saviour**'. The fish also symbolizes baptism by water, spiritual nourishment and life. Early Christians were sometimes called 'pisculi' (fish) by important men within the Christian **Church** who were known as Fathers.

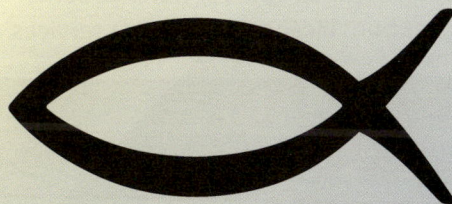

How Christians use symbols

In this section you will:

● find out more about Christian symbols

● look at some of the ways Christians use symbols to express their religious feelings, beliefs and ideas

● learn about a Christian **denomination** called the Salvation Army and its symbols.

Christians use symbolism in a variety of ways. They have different views about the value of using symbols in their religion. Some denominations deliberately keep symbolism to a minimum because they think that symbols can distract people and take their attention away from God. Other Christian groups believe that symbols can help people to focus on God and they have an important role to play in their faith. Symbolism affects the shape of **church** buildings and the objects inside. It affects the way people worship and how they dress for religious purposes. It also affects the language they use and the way they describe God.

Some churches have been built in the shape of a **cross**, the main symbol of Christianity. Symbols can be an important part of worship. Some churches burn **incense** during their services.

Some churches, such as the Greek Orthodox Church, burn incense during their services

This creates atmosphere and the rising smoke represents prayers ascending to God. Churches are often decorated with flowers. This shows that God is special and they are symbols of love and devotion. Worshippers also light candles. The candle as a source of light symbolizes goodness, knowledge and truth.

Christians call Jesus the 'Light of the World' because they believe that he overcame the darkness of ignorance and evil and showed people the right way to live. Christians often use non-literal or symbolic language to describe Jesus or God. They do this because they believe that it is very difficult to say exactly what God is like so they use symbolism to express their ideas and beliefs about God. For example, Christians often refer to God as 'Father'. They don't literally believe that God is their father but they do believe that He behaves like a caring father towards them.

The way Christians act during worship can be symbolic. Some Christians bend their right knee and bow when they pass in front of the altar, as they enter or leave the church. This is called **genuflection** and symbolizes respect for God. The positions Christians adopt whilst praying are also symbolic. Kneeling down and the bowing of heads whilst praying are symbols of **humility**. The worshipper is acknowledging that God is much greater than they are. Likewise, standing up to pray shows respect. Sometimes Christians prostrate or lay themselves on the ground whilst praying. This gesture shows that they are submitting to or prepared to follow the will of God. It also symbolizes their belief that they are dependent or reliant on God.

During some services, as a symbol of peace, Christians put their arms around each other or shake hands. At other times, the **priest** places their hands on a person's head or body as a symbol of God's blessing and healing. This action is known as the 'laying on of hands'.

Members of the Salvation Army

The colour of **vestments**, special clothes worn by priests during worship, and soft church furnishings like the altar frontals, a decorative hanging in front of the altar, are symbolic and are changed throughout the course of a year. Colour is also associated with certain services and ceremonies. People being baptized, confirmed and a Christian bride traditionally wears white which symbolizes purity. Similarly, the mourners at a funeral sometimes wear black or dark clothing to symbolize their sadness and grief.

Clothing can also have symbolic meaning. For example, a **priest** will wear a clerical collar, usually called a 'dog collar'. The collar resembles the iron halters which were fixed around the necks of slaves. It symbolizes that priests are not their own master but do the work of God. Monks and nuns, Christians who belong to religious orders, also wear clothes which symbolize their way of life and commitment to God, as do the members of the **Salvation Army**. Christians who belong to this denomination wear a smart uniform. This symbolizes their belief that the Christian faith requires them to live a disciplined and orderly life.

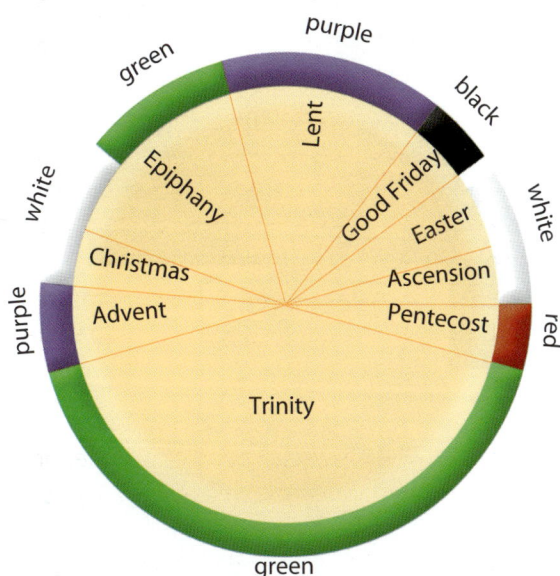

The Christian church has different seasons, represented by various colours

The Salvation Army

The Salvation Army was founded in the East End of London by William Booth.

In 1878 CE, Captain William Ebden designed a crest for the organization which is full of symbolism.

The cross, the symbol of the Christian faith, is at the centre of the crest. It has an 'S' wrapped around it, which represents **salvation** through the death of Jesus. The two crossed swords represent the battle against sin. The rays surrounding the central image are reminders of fire and light associated with the **Holy Spirit**. The roundels are shots which represents the truth of the gospels. The crown represents the glory or reward God which will give to his faithful followers.

'Blood and Fire' is the Salvation Army's motto. It refers to the death and sacrifice of Jesus and the power of the Holy Spirit.

Worship

In this section you will:

- learn about Christian worship
- discover why Christians worship God
- study the main features of a Christian church
- gain an understanding of some of the main features found inside Roman Catholic and some Anglican churches.

Worship means paying special attention to something. When **Christians** worship they show that God is important to them. Worshipping God is central to Christianity. Christians worship God for one or more of the following reasons:

- to show their love for God
- to demonstrate their commitment to God
- to thank or praise God
- to ask God for help or guidance in their daily lives
- to ask God for forgiveness
- to strengthen their faith and become closer to God.

Where do Christians worship?

Christians can worship together in public or on their own in private. The main day on which Christians gather together to worship God is on a Sunday. Sunday is the Christian **holy** day. The word 'holy' means 'to do with God'. One reason why Christians have set Sunday aside as a special day of rest and worship is because this is the day on which they believe Jesus rose from the dead. Christians worship God in a variety of buildings such as a private home, abbey, chapel, cathedral, minster, citadel and **church**.

The majority of Christians worship God in a church. There are thousands of Christian churches throughout the world. In Christianity, the word 'church' has several meanings. 'Church' with a capital 'C' refers to different **denominations** or the worldwide Christian community. The word 'church' with a small 'c' refers to the building in which many Christians worship.

A church is regarded as a sacred place. Christians treat their place of worship and the objects in it with great respect.

Features of a Christian place of worship

Traditionally, churches were designed in the shape of a **cross**, the main symbol of Christianity. They were built facing east in the direction of the rising sun. The rising sun marks the beginning of a new day. It is a source of light and life and symbolizes the Christian belief in

Pulpit - a raised platform from where the clergy give a **sermon** to the **congregation**.

Chancel – the front area of the church.

Choir stalls

Altar or Holy Table – a raised table where the **Eucharist** or Holy Communion takes place.

Vestry – a room where the official clothing of the clergy are kept, along with robes that the choir wear.

Nave – this is where the congregation sit. They sit on seats called **pews**.

Lectern – a stand on which the Bible is placed when it is read out loud.

Side chapel – a small section of the church which has its own altar. It is used for private prayer or special services.

Font – The font is a large stone container which holds holy water. It is where people, usually infants, are baptized.

Pews

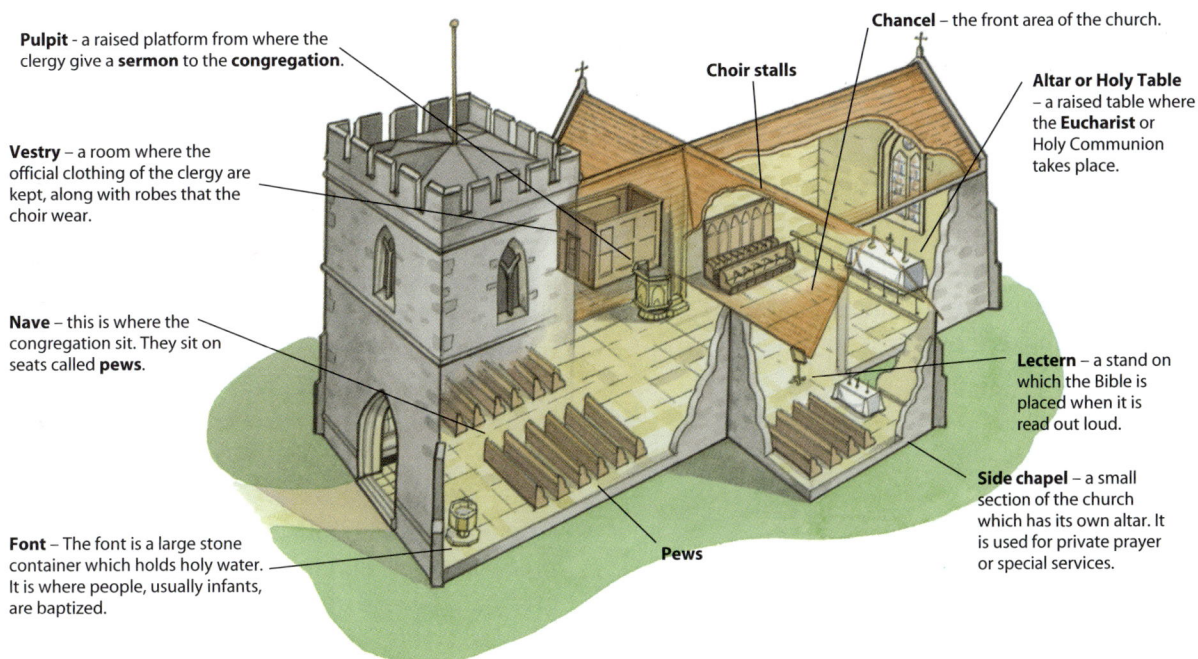

The main features of an Anglican church

Jesus' **resurrection**. East is also the direction of Jerusalem, the place where Christians believe Jesus died and rose from the dead. Modern churches have been built in many different shapes and sizes and in a variety of locations. Christians have also adapted other buildings and made them into churches.

Modern churches sometimes have the altar in the centre of the church. This reflects the involvement of the laity, ordinary members of the congregation.

Roman Catholic churches usually have the same features as traditional Anglican churches but they also have some additional characteristics.

The stoup

The stoup is a small basin containing **holy** water, placed inside the main entrance to Roman Catholic and some Anglican churches. Worshippers entering the church will dip their fingers into the stoup and make the sign of the cross on themselves.

The tabernacle and confessional

The tabernacle is found in Roman Catholic churches and in some Anglican churches. It is a cupboard made out of cloth and contains bread or wafers that have been **consecrated** (made holy), ready for use during the **Eucharist**.

A confessional is found in Roman Catholic churches. It is either a small room or two cubicles linked by a grille, which means that you can hear but not see the person on the other side. Worshippers use them to confess their sins anonymously to a **priest**.

Ways of worshipping

How do Christians worship?

There are two different styles of **Christian** worship. Some Christians prefer to worship God in a formal or structured way. This is called liturgical worship. Liturgical worship involves following a set pattern of rituals called a **liturgy**. This kind of worship is colourful, dramatic and full of symbolism. Worshippers express many of their beliefs by using symbolic objects and performing symbolic actions. Most Churches have their liturgies written down in a book which worshippers follow during services.

Other Christians choose to worship God in a less formal and unstructured way. They have fewer rituals and use less symbolism. This is called non-liturgical worship. In non-liturgical worship the emphasis is on the written or spoken word. Hymns, prayers, Bible readings, **sermons** and personal testimonies are important. This form of worship is found in **Protestant** churches. The Anglican Church, however, uses liturgical worship.

Many Christians believe that worship should not just be confined to church. They think that their everyday lives should be an act of worship. This means praising and being thankful to God in everything they do. Christians say that even the most ordinary things they do take on new meaning when they remember God.

The Eucharist

The most important set service or liturgy is the **Eucharist**. During this service Christians remember the final meal Jesus had with his disciples now called the **Last Supper**. They share a symbolic meal of bread and wine together and reflect upon Jesus' death. The bread symbolizes his body and the wine represents his blood. Different **denominations** call the Eucharist by different names and celebrate it in various ways. They also have different beliefs about what happens to the bread and wine during the ceremony. Many Christians believe that it actually becomes the body and blood of Jesus and he is therefore really present during the service. This idea is known as **transubstantiation**.

The Eucharist is a **sacrament**. A sacrament is an event or experience where Christians believe they receive special blessings from God. Seven activities are regarded as sacraments: **baptism**, Eucharist (also known as **Holy Communion**), **confirmation**, **marriage**, **confession**, **ordination** and **Anointing of the Sick**. Sacraments are particularly important to Roman Catholics.

Aids to worship

Different denominations use different things to help them worship. This table shows the variety of things Christians might use during worship.

Incense
Incense creates atmosphere. It is a sweet smelling gum or spice which gives off odour and smoke when burnt. The incense container or censer is swung from a chain during worship. The smoke rises and this represents prayers which are making their way to God.

Music
A wide range of musical instruments are used during worship. Music is used as an accompaniment to hymns, prayers, **psalms** and other religious songs.

Singing

Worshippers also express their ideas, feelings and beliefs by singing hymns, prayers, psalms and other religious songs. In some Churches there is no musical accompaniment. Orthodox Christians believe that the human voice is the finest thing to use when worshipping God and nothing must detract from this.

Silence

Periods of silence can help the worshipper to concentrate and focus on God.

Candles

A variety of candles are lit during worship. They represent the goodness and light of God which shines in a dark and sinful world.

Cross and crucifix

The **cross** is the symbol of Christianity. It helps Christians to focus and reminds them of Jesus' resurrection. A crucifix is a cross with a figure of Jesus on it.

Bread and wine

Christians share bread and wine together during some services. Jesus asked his disciples to do this in memory of him. The bread represents Jesus' body and the wine his blood.

Icons

An icon is a holy picture representing Jesus, the **Virgin Mary** or another **saint**. They help Christians to focus on God. Worshippers pray and place lit candles in front of icons. They believe that Jesus and saints like the Virgin Mary are already in the presence of God and they hope that they will intercede on their behalf and help them to communicate with God. Icons are mainly used by Orthodox Christians and are objects of great devotion. They are carried in processions during festivals.

Statues

Christians focus on statues of saints like the Virgin Mary, the mother of Jesus, during worship. Worshippers pray and place lit candles in front of statues. They believe that Jesus and saints like the Virgin Mary are already in the presence of God and they hope that they will intercede on their behalf and help them to communicate with God.

Actions

Worshippers express their ideas, feelings and beliefs by performing certain actions such as clapping, dancing, kneeling and genuflecting. They might also put their arms around each other or shake hands as a sign of peace.

The Bible

Passages from the Bible are read during most services.

Service book

A service book sets out the order of service. It tells the worshipper what to do and say.

Rosary

A rosary is a string of beads with a crucifix attached. They are mainly used by Roman Catholics who pass the beads between their thumb and forefinger whilst they are praying.

The Eucharist service

The following things usually happen during most Eucharist celebrations. The first part of the service concentrates on words associated with God and the Christian faith. This might include: hymns, prayers of preparation, penitence, absolution and intercession, Bible readings, an affirmation of faith and a sermon.

The next part of the service focuses on the Eucharist. The priest talks about the Last Supper, and places the bread and wine on the **altar** or **holy** table where it is **consecrated** (made holy) with a special prayer. Another important prayer of thanksgiving, called the Eucharist Prayer, is said, and the bread and wine is shared out amongst the congregation. The way in which worshippers receive communion (bread and wine) varies according to the denomination. In the Church of England, worshippers usually kneel at the altar, where they are given a thin wafer of bread and take a sip of wine from a chalice.

At the end of the service there is a final hymn, some closing prayers and a blessing. Christians are also reminded of their duty to serve others.

Prayer

In this section you will:

- learn about Christian prayer

- find out how and why Christians pray and look at different forms of prayer

- read and reflect upon some important Christian prayers, such as the Lord's Prayer.

Christians believe that you can develop a personal relationship with God. One way they do this is through **prayer**. Prayer is a way of communicating with God. It involves talking and listening to God. Many Christians look upon God as their best friend and prayer is a very important part of their everyday life and worship.

How and why do Christians pray?

Christians pray in various ways. They can pray on their own or in a group. Prayers can be said spontaneously on the spur of the moment or at set times. They can be said out loud or silently inside a person's head. Christians can adopt various positions for prayer. Sometimes they kneel down, put their hands together and close their eyes. At other times they might sit or stand.

Christians pray for a variety of reasons. One of the main reasons Christians pray is to improve their relationship with God. They also pray because they believe that prayer can change things. Christians believe in the 'power of prayer'. The following are examples of why Christians say they pray.

Christians are taught to love and pray for their enemies (Matthew 5: 44)

'One of the reasons I pray is:

…because I want God to know that I love him

…to let God know that he is important to me

…to say sorry for the things I have done wrong and ask God to forgive me

…to try and be a better person

… to ask for guidance

…to gain strength if I am having a difficult time

…to ask for help for myself and others

…because I can't help it. Something inside me just makes me want to talk to God

…because Jesus told us to

…to say thank you to God for all the good things in my life

… to find out what God wants me to do.'

What kind of prayers do Christians use?

There are five main forms of prayer which Christians use:

1. Adoration – the person praying focuses on God's greatness and power. They think about how special and important God is.

2. Confession – the person praying focuses on what God expects of them. They think about the things they have done wrong and ask God for forgiveness.

3. Intercession – the person praying focuses on the needs of others. They think about people who need help or guidance and ask God to assist them.

4. Petition – the person praying focuses on their personal needs. They ask God for help and guidance.

5. Thanksgiving – the person praying focuses on God's love and generosity. They think about what God has done for them and say thank you.

Meditation is another form of prayer. It is a quiet form of praying. The person praying is still and silent. They focus on God and try very hard not to think about anything else.

Christians can make up their own prayers or they can use prayers which have been written by other people. One of the most well-known Christian prayers is the Lord's Prayer. This prayer is found in the **Gospels** in Matthew 6: 9–13. Christians believe that Jesus taught this prayer to his disciples. It is used during most acts of Christian worship.

Christian prayers

Many Christian prayers express what it means to be a Christian. For Christians, this means knowing, loving and following Jesus. It means recognizing the sacrifice that Jesus made for them and what he achieved. It also involves behaving in the way that Jesus would want. The following prayer, by Richard of Chichester (1197–1253 CE), has been made famous by the song 'Day by Day' in the religious musical *Godspell*.

Thanks be to thee, my Lord Jesus Christ,
For all the benefits thou hast won for me,
For all the pains and insults thou hast borne for me.
O most merciful **Redeemer**, Friend and Brother,
May I know thee more clearly,
Love thee more dearly,
And follow thee more nearly;
For ever and ever.

An important theme in modern Christian prayers is international justice.

O God,
To those who have hunger, give bread;
And to us who have bread, give the hunger for justice.

Latin American prayer

Festivals

In this section you will:
- gain an understanding of festivals and why they are important
- learn about the main Christian festivals
- find out when they occur and what they commemorate.

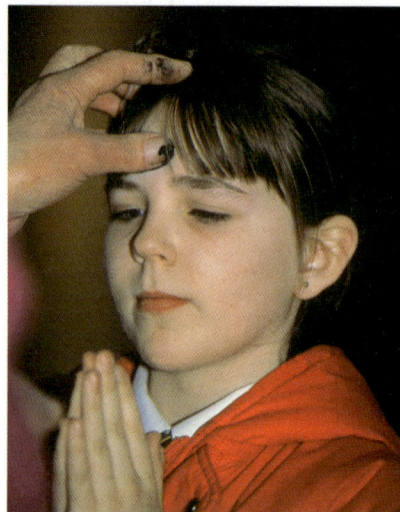

A cross of ash is made on a young worshipper's forehead

Festivals usually celebrate or commemorate a significant event. Most festivals remember an event in the past but they can also look to the future like the Chinese New Year. Festivals can be religious or **secular** occasions.

The main **Christian** festivals are based on significant events in Jesus' life. The date of Christian festivals can change, only Christmas and Epiphany fall on the same date each year. This is because festival dates are determined by the date of **Easter Day** which is always the Sunday after the full moon in March. The exact date of Easter can vary by several weeks.

Epiphany – 6 January

Epiphany remembers how the Magi or Wise Men from the East came to visit the newborn baby Jesus. The Magi were the first Gentiles (non-Jews) to visit Jesus. This festival celebrates them recognizing his special status. Epiphany marks the end of the Christmas period. Traditionally, it is the day when all the Christmas decorations should be taken down and put away.

Ash Wednesday – February/March

Ash Wednesday is a day of humility and penitence. It is a time when Christians show they are sorry for the things they have done wrong. One way some of them do this is by going to a special church service where the **priest** smears a cross of ash on their foreheads. The ash comes from the burning of the previous year's palm crosses, crosses made from palm leaves which are given to worshippers on **Palm Sunday**. Ash Wednesday also marks the beginning of Lent, a time of fasting and prayer in preparation for Easter.

Easter – March/April

Easter is the most important festival in the Christian Church. It begins on **Good Friday** when Christians commemorate the suffering and death of Jesus and ends on Easter Sunday when they celebrate their belief in his **resurrection**.

Ascension Day – May/June

Ascension Day is when Christians celebrate their belief that Jesus left the earth and ascended (went up) into the presence of God 40 days after his resurrection. The state of being with God after death is known as Heaven.

Trinity Sunday – May/June

Trinity Sunday is when Christians celebrate their belief in the Trinity. The Trinity is the Christian idea that there is one God who has made Himself known to the world in three ways: Father, Son and Holy Spirit.

Christmas – 25 December

Christmas is a twelve-day celebration which commemorates the birth of Jesus. No one knows exactly when Jesus was born. About 300 years after Jesus' death, Christians took over a mid-winter **pagan** festival and dedicated it to Jesus' birth.

'…He was taken up to Heaven as they watched him…' (Acts 1: 9)

Pentecost – May/June

At Pentecost Christians celebrate the giving of the **Holy Spirit** to Jesus' followers and the founding of the Christian Church. In the **New Testament** it says that just before Jesus ascended to heaven he promised his disciples that God would send them a helper. This helper was called the Holy Spirit, who would support and guide them. The New Testament also says that ten days later whilst the early Christians were celebrating the Jewish festival of Shavuot (Feast of Weeks), there was a gushing wind and flames of fire and the Holy Spirit came amongst them. This made them realize that they must spread the 'Good News' about Jesus. Christians look upon this event as the official beginning or the birthday of the Christian Church.

In this country, Pentecost is also known as Whitsun or 'White Sunday'. This is because it became a popular day for baptisms and the people entering the Christian Church wore white as a symbol of purity.

The Transfiguration

The Transfiguration is a festival which is very important for Orthodox Christians. It is held in August and commemorates the belief that Jesus was transformed or altered in some way when he went up a high mountain with three of his disciples.

The **Gospels** also state that whilst Jesus was on the mountain he spoke with Moses and Elijah (two very important Jews who had died). While he was talking, a shining cloud came over them, and a voice from the cloud said, 'This is my own dear Son with whom I am pleased – listen to him!' (Matthew 17: 5) Many Christians believe that this was God speaking and that this event confirms the **divine** nature of Jesus.

Christmas and Easter

In this section you will:

● learn what the festivals of Easter and Christmas mean to Christians and find out how they prepare for and celebrate Christmas

● read about and reflect upon St Nicholas, one of the most important Christian **saints**.

Easter and Christmas are the two most important festivals in Christianity.

Christmas remembers Jesus' birth and celebrates the **Incarnation**. Christmas is also a time of thanksgiving. **Christians** think that, through Jesus, God gave himself to the world. He became involved in the lives of human beings and changed things for the better.

Easter is the most significant of all Christian festivals. It remembers Jesus' death and celebrates the Christian belief that Jesus rose from the dead. The events of Easter honour Jesus and remind Christians of who he was and what he did for them. Easter also gives Christians hope for the future. It celebrates the Christian belief that there is life after death and that good always triumphs over evil.

Christians understand Jesus' life and death in a particular way. They think that his life and death had a purpose. Christians believe that Jesus made it possible for human beings to have a close personal relationship with God. They say that before Jesus was born human beings had forgotten about God and the way He or She wanted them to live. People lived according to their own selfish desires and committed many sins. Christians say that Jesus changed things.

He reminded people about God and taught them the right way to live. Jesus also put right the wrongs of the past. Christians believe that

Jesus' death made up or atoned for the sins of human beings and reconciled or brought together human beings and God. This is why the day Jesus died is called **Good Friday** because something very good happened as a result of his death.

The **resurrection** has several meanings for Christians. Most importantly, they believe it proves that Jesus was the Son of God and that he is alive today. It is also seen as a sign of God's **forgiveness** and proof that life continues after death.

Jesus is often called **Redeemer** because he redeemed or 'brought back' people to God. Jesus is also referred to as a **Saviour** because he saved people from the consequences of their sin and death. **Atonement**, **Redemption**, **Reconciliation**, **Salvation** and **Eternal Life** are important ideas in Christianity.

How do Christians celebrate Christmas?

The four weeks before Christmas are known as Advent. The word 'advent' means 'coming'. Advent is a period of preparation before Christmas. During Advent, Christians think about Jesus coming to the world as a baby and what this meant for human beings. Christians believe that Jesus was the **Messiah**, a saviour sent by God to bring goodness and peace to the Earth.

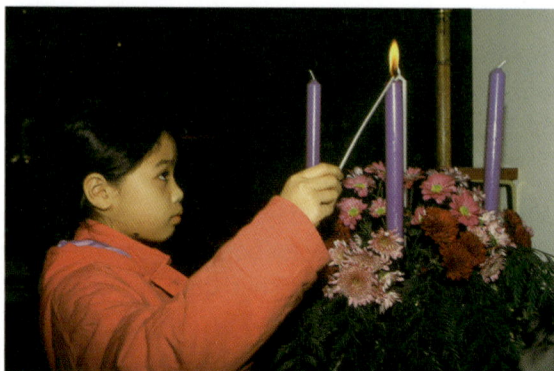

Counting the days until Christmas

Christians enjoy celebrating Christmas, but they also think carefully about the meaning of the festival

Christians also read and reflect upon passages from the Bible which talk about the Messiah and what He will be like. Another thing Christians think about is the future, as they believe Jesus promised his disciples that he would return to Earth one day to judge people and to decide who should go to Heaven. This is known as the **Second Coming** as it will be the second time Jesus has been to Earth.

Carols are a sung throughout the Christmas period. A carol is a hymn about Jesus' birth. Some Christians light Advent candles and use Advent calendars to count the days to Christmas Day. Houses and many churches are also decorated with Christmas trees and coloured lights. Light is used a lot at Christmas. This represents the Christian belief that Jesus is the light of the world. Christmas is sometimes called a festival of light because it celebrates the birth of Jesus whom Christians call 'light of the world'. Christians also believe that Jesus was God's gift to the world. This is where the idea of people giving and receiving presents comes from.

Most Christians try to go to church at Christmas and take part in the **Eucharist**. One of the most popular services at Christmas is called the **Midnight Mass** which begins at about 11.30pm on Christmas Eve.

What do Christians say about Christmas?

'…Many people have forgotten the real meaning of Christmas … it's not about tinsel, selection boxes and presents … it's about Jesus!'

'…I especially try to follow Jesus' example at Christmas … I think about people who are less fortunate than myself and try to help them.'

'…I love all the lights of Christmas … I think light is a good way to represent Jesus because his goodness shines and stands out against the darkness of evil.'

St Nicholas

St Nicholas is a popular Christian saint. There are nearly 500 **churches** dedicated to him in Britain alone. His feast day is on 6 December and is celebrated by most Christian Churches. St Nicholas is associated with generosity, kindness and protecting the rights of the innocent. He is the patron saint of children, and there are many legends and myths associated with him, particularly about Christmas.

The tradition of hanging up stockings on Christmas Eve comes from a story about St Nicholas. A poor man had no money to give to his daughters on their wedding day. So St Nicholas, who liked to help people anonymously, dropped bags of gold down the chimney of their house. The gold fell into stockings which the girls had left to dry by the fire. Children have hung up stockings on Christmas Eve ever since hoping that they will be filled with presents.

Easter

In this section you will:

● find out how Christians prepare for and celebrate Easter

● look at what some Christians say about Easter

● learn about the ways in which some Christian communities celebrate Easter with colourful carnival parades.

A Palm Sunday procession

How do Christians celebrate Easter?

Traditionally, **Christians** begin preparing for Easter on Shrove Tuesday, the day before Ash Wednesday, the beginning of Lent. Shrove Tuesday is also known as 'Pancake Day'. It is called 'Pancake Day' because in the past Christians followed a very strict diet during Lent and didn't eat any rich foods. Foods such as eggs, milk and flour were considered luxuries so they were used up to make pancakes before the Lenten fast began. Today, most Christians try to give up something they usually enjoy eating for Lent, such as chocolate.

Lent lasts for 40 days and ends on Easter Sunday. It lasts for this amount of time because Christianity teaches that Jesus spent 40 days and nights in the desert being tempted by the Devil before he began his ministry. Lent is a solemn and serious time for the Christian **Church**. Some Churches have traditions which symbolize this like flowers being taken out of the church and the covering up of icons and other religious objects.

The last week of Lent is known as **Holy Week**. This is when Christians remember the final seven days of Jesus' life. It begins with **Palm Sunday** and includes **Maundy Thursday**, **Good Friday** and **Holy Saturday**.

According to the **New Testament**, Jesus came to Jerusalem to celebrate the Jewish festival of **Pesach** (Passover). He rode on a donkey and was welcomed by people waving palm leaves and placing them in his path. Palm Sunday is when Christians commemorate Jesus' entry into Jerusalem. Many churches hand out **crosses** made of palm leaves in memory of this event.

Maundy Thursday is when Christians remember the final meal or **Last Supper** Jesus had with his disciples and his arrest in the Garden of Gethsemane. In some Christian communities the **priest** will wash the feet of his or her congregation. This reminds worshippers of the sacrifice Jesus made and demonstrates the Christian belief that everyone is equal in the eyes of God.

Russian Orthodox Christians kiss the coffin of Christ on Good Friday

Good Friday is when Christians mourn the death of Jesus. It the saddest day in the Christian year. Churches are stripped of their usual decorations and the colour of soft furnishings, like the altar frontals, are changed to black. Many Christians spend between 12.00pm and 3.00pm, the time Jesus is believed to have spent on the cross, in church meditating on the suffering and death of Jesus. Some Christians also take part in processions and the Orthodox Church holds a kind of funeral for Jesus.

Holy Saturday is the last day of Lent. During the day, churches are cleaned and decorated with flowers, in preparation for **Easter Day**. Christians attend a late evening service called the Easter Vigil. The word 'vigil' means 'to keep watch' and worshippers wait expectantly for Easter Day to arrive. The service starts in darkness, with the exception of a few candles so that the Bible can be read. Gradually, the church becomes filled with light as worshippers light candles from the **paschal candle**. The paschal candle represents the light of Jesus; and the change from darkness to light represents the Christian belief that Jesus overcame death and good triumphed over evil.

Easter Sunday is when Christians celebrate their belief that Jesus came back to life after he died. This is known as the resurrection and there are many traditions and customs associated with this important Christian event. It is a very joyful occasion and Christians make a special effort to go to church and take part in the **Eucharist**. Some Churches begin the day with a bonfire at dawn. They also hard boil eggs and paint them. The eggs are symbols of new life. Chocolate Easter eggs, which many people enjoy eating, have developed from this idea.

What do Christians say about Easter?

'…On Good Friday I mourn Jesus. I feel His pain and suffering. On Easter Sunday I feel happy. I know that Jesus is alive and I celebrate His victory over death.'

'…Easter reminds me that there is life after death … I think about people I have known who have died … and I feel happy to think that I will see them again one day.'

'…Easter is a time of new beginnings … Jesus sacrificed himself so that we could have a fresh start with God.'

'Easter reminds me that with God everything is possible … the Holy Spirit brought Jesus back to life … imagine what it can do for ordinary people!'

Mardi Gras

Some Roman Catholic communities like to make the most of the week before Lent. A series of carnival days called Mardi Gras (French for 'Fat Tuesday') are held in places such as New Orleans (USA), Rio de Janeiro (Brazil), Nice (France) and Cologne (Germany). Mardi Gras have spectacular parades featuring floats, pageants, elaborate costumes, masked balls and dancing in the streets.

The word carnival comes from an Old Italian word, 'carnelevare', which means the removal of meat. This refers to the fast observed by some Christians during Lent, when they do not eat any meat for six weeks.

Mother's Day

The fourth Sunday in Lent is Mothering Sunday. Traditionally, this was a time when people who worked as servants away from home were given time off to visit their 'mother' church in the parish where they lived, and they would also visit their mothers.

Pilgrimage 1

In this section you will:

● learn about Christian pilgrimage

● find out why Christians might go on a pilgrimage and look at some of the sites they could visit

● read and reflect upon the fourth-century pilgrimage of Egeria.

A **pilgrimage** is a religious journey. It is also a form of worship. A person who goes on a pilgrimage is called a **pilgrim**. Pilgrims visit places they believe to be holy or sacred. A place is usually considered holy or sacred if something of religious importance has happened there, such as a miraculous event or the birth of a leader or teacher. Sites of pilgrimage can be found in a variety of locations. People can make pilgrimages on their own or go with others.

People go on pilgrimages for different reasons:

● to strengthen their faith and become closer to God

● to show commitment to their religion

● to say thank you for something good which has happened

● to make up for something they have done wrong (**penance**)

● to ask for help or healing

● to fulfil their religious duty

● to follow tradition or to satisfy their curiosity.

Most people think of pilgrimage as an actual physical journey to a particular place. It can also refer to our journey through life from birth to death. Another understanding of pilgrimage is that it can refer to an inner journey. An inner journey is the process by which we learn more about ourselves as we grow and develop.

One of the ways **Christians** find out more about themselves, and what they believe God wants of them, is by going on a retreat. When Christians go on retreat they take a break from their normal lives. They stay in a quiet and peaceful place and spend time thinking and praying.

Where do Christians go on pilgrimage?

There are many Christian holy sites all over the world. Most are 'official' sites of pilgrimage. This means that the Christian Church has accepted that something special has happened there. There are also 'unofficial' sites of pilgrimage where people claim extraordinary and supernatural things have taken place but they are not officially recognized by the Church.

The Holy Land

The tomb of Christ in the Church of the Holy Sepulchre, Jerusalem, is an important pilgrimage site for Christians

Israel is the country where Jesus lived. It is also known as the Holy Land because it contains many holy sites. Israel is a very popular place of pilgrimage. Pilgrims like to (literally) follow in the footsteps of Jesus and visit the places associated with him. These include Bethlehem, the town where he was born, Nazareth where Jesus grew up and Jerusalem, the place of his crucifixion and **resurrection**.

Rome

Rome in Italy is an important pilgrimage site for Christians as it was a centre for the early Church. Many of the early Christians, including the **apostles** Peter and Paul, were martyred there. Pilgrims can visit the Catacombs, underground burial chambers where the early Christians used to meet and worship in secret. Pilgrims can also see the Vatican and St Peter's Basilica. The Vatican is the home of the Pope, the leader of the Roman Catholic Church. St Peter's Basilica is very a beautiful church dedicated to Peter who was the first Pope. The church was built on the site of Peter's grave and there is a **shrine** inside dedicated to him.

Lourdes

Millions of pilgrims visit Lourdes every year to pray and receive healing

Another famous place of pilgrimage is Lourdes in France. Lourdes is where a fourteen-year-old French girl called Bernadette Soubirous is believed to have seen the **Virgin Mary**, Jesus' mother, in 1858. The **apparition** appeared in a grotto near the banks of a river. She emphasized the importance of **prayer** and **penance** and requested that a chapel be built. The Virgin Mary also told Bernadette to dig in the mud. A spring appeared which is believed to have healing properties. Many people claim to have been miraculously cured from serious illnesses or disabilities after bathing in the spring.

Egeria's travels

Hundreds of Europeans set out on pilgrimages to the Holy Land in 385–1099 CE. Eighteen pilgrims wrote accounts of their journeys.

A lady called Egeria made one of the earliest recorded pilgrimages to the Holy Land during the fourth century CE. She wrote an account of her travels and described in great detail holy places associated with Jesus, particularly Jerusalem. Egeria also provided important information about the way in which the early Church worshipped and how it was organized.

Egeria's journal shows that she was very devoted to God. It records that she and her companions stopped at each stage of their pilgrimage, gave thanks to the Lord and read biblical passages relevant to their location.

'When I had arrived there, I went through all the churches – that of the Apostles and all the martyr-memorials, of which there are very many – and I ceased not to give thanks to Jesus our God, Who had thus deigned to bestow His mercy upon me.'

Pilgrimage 2

In this section you will:

- look at some sites of Christian pilgrimage
- read and reflect upon the Taizé community in France which offers a place of retreat for Christians.

Fatima

Fatima, in Portugal, is a very popular Roman Catholic **pilgrimage** site. Fatima is where three children, Lucia de Jesus, aged ten, and her cousins Francisco and Jacinta Marto, aged nine and seven, are believed to have seen the **Virgin Mary** in 1917. The **apparition**, who was described as a 'Lady more brilliant than the sun', emphasized the importance of **prayer** and **penance**. She also told Lucia three secrets called the Secrets of Fatima. The first secret was a vision of hell, believed to refer to the two world wars. The second secret was a vision of peace.

Only part of the third secret has been revealed. The Vatican, the centre of authority for the Roman Catholic Church, says that it involves martyrdom and suffering. It has been linked with the failed assassination attempt on Pope John Paul II in 1981.

Pilgrims visiting Fatima sometimes approach the shrine on their knees as a penance. This shows that they are sorry for the things they have done wrong. They also buy and light large candles, which they place in a big furnace. The candles are usually lit for someone or something and a prayer is said as they are put into the fire.

Walsingham

Some people regard Walsingham in Norfolk as an **ecumenical** pilgrimage site. This is because **Christians** from different **denominations** go there on pilgrimage. Walsingham is where Richeldis de Faverches is believed to have had a vision of the Virgin Mary in 1061. The apparition showed her Jesus' home in Nazareth and Richeldis built a replica of the house she had seen. When Christians visit the Holy House they think about Jesus' childhood and adolescence. It also reminds them of the **Incarnation**. The Holy House represents the important Christian belief that Jesus was the Son of God but he also had a human mother and family.

Medjugorje

Medjugorje in Bosnia is a modern unofficial pilgrimage site. Since 1981, six young people who live in this village claim to have seen more than 300 visions of the Virgin Mary. The visionaries say that the Virgin Mary's purpose for coming to Earth is to guide people back to God. She is also believed to have left behind proof of her visitations in the form of miraculously appearing images. Many Christians visit Medjugorje in the hope of finding peace. The word 'Medjugorje' means 'between the hills'. It has been described as a 'place where Heaven touches the Earth'.

Many retreats are held in Christian settings such as a monastery or abbey

Iona

Iona is a small island off the west coast of Scotland. It is a place of pilgrimage and retreat. Iona was originally the home of St Columba, an Irish Christian prince. He established a monastery there when he was forced to leave Ireland in 563 CE. Today, Iona is an ecumenical Christian community with 240 members from a variety of backgrounds and denominations. Iona is a symbol of Christian unity. It shows that different Christian groups can live, work and worship together.

Members of the community don't have to spend all of their time on Iona but they do need to follow the 'rules' of the community wherever they are. They must:

- take part in regular acts of worship (which includes praying for half an hour each morning)

- be prepared to share what they have with others

- account for the way they use their time and money

- meet with other members of the community (three times on the mainland and for a week in the summer on Iona)

- work for justice and peace.

Ordinary Christians can spend time on Iona either as volunteers, employees or pilgrims on retreat. The community also runs a youth organization and young people can stay on the island during their holidays. Most people who have visited Iona agree that it is a beautiful and special place. They come back home feeling rested and closer to God.

Taizé

Taizé is an ecumenical Christian community of monks in a small village in Eastern France. It was founded by Brother Roger in 1940. His aim was to unite Christians and overcome conflict within the Christian faith.

Today, hundreds of thousands of young adults from every continent visit Taizé to pray and to help prepare themselves to work for peace, reconciliation and trust throughout the world. Many visitors stay for a week and live as part of the community. They can choose several ways of spending the week, including being silent. Taizé welcomes young people who do not consider themselves believers and occasionally people from other faiths come, too.

Prayer is an important part of daily routine in the Taizé community, as is singing and discussion. A typical day starts with prayers at 8.20a.m. and ends with prayers at 8.30p.m.

Baptism

42

In this section you will:

- gain an understanding of what a rite of passage means
- learn about the Christian rites of passage
- find out why baptism is important to Christians and what happens during an infant baptism
- read about and reflect upon what it means to be baptized into the Church of England.

Believers' baptisms are happy and joyous occasions

Many **Christians** look upon life as a pilgrimage. They say that life is a journey from the 'cradle to the grave'. Christians believe that they are given life by God at the beginning of their time on Earth and return to God at the end. **Rites of passage** are special ceremonies which mark important events along the way. They are called rites of passage because the ceremonies have rituals (or rites) which are associated with the passing of time on Earth.

The four main Christian rites of passage are **baptism**, **confirmation**, **marriage** and **death**. Baptism, confirmation and marriage and are also known as **sacraments** by many Christians. A sacrament is an event or experience where Christians believe they receive special blessings from God.

Baptism

Christians think that **baptism** is important because it is the ceremony by which people enter the Christian faith and become members of the Christian **Church**. The **Gospels** say that Jesus was baptized in the River Jordan by his cousin, John the Baptist. They also say that Jesus asked his followers to be baptized.

Christians believe that by being baptized they are following Jesus' example and doing what he asked. Jesus' baptism marks the beginning of his public ministry. When Christians are baptized it marks the beginning of their life as a Christian.

What happens during baptism?

Some **denominations** baptize people when they are babies. This is known as **infant baptism**. Another name for baptism is christening. The word 'christening' comes from the idea of being given a name in Christ (as a Christian). This is because part of the baptism ceremony involves being given a Christian name.

Baptism takes place in a church. It can be part of an ordinary service or a private ceremony. Traditionally, the baby is dressed in white as a symbol of purity and goodness.

Parents and godparents gather round the font and take vows on the baby's behalf and promise to help bring them up in the Christian faith. The parents name the child and the vicar or **priest** makes the sign of the **cross** on the baby's forehead. **Holy water** is poured from the font onto the baby's head three times, once for each member of the **Trinity**: Father, Son and **Holy Spirit**.

This method of baptism is known as affusion. Water is a very important symbol during baptism. This is because Christianity teaches that everyone is born in a state of **sin**. This belief is called the doctrine of original sin. The doctrine of original sin is based on the idea that the very first human beings disobeyed God and their sins have been passed on to every human being since. When water is poured on the baby it represents spiritual cleansing, the idea of washing away sins and starting again. This means that the baby can no longer be blamed for things human beings have done wrong before it was born. In Roman Catholic baptisms the baby is also anointed with oil on the chest and head. During Orthodox baptisms the baby (or adult) is completely immersed in water three times which symbolizes a belief in the Trinity, the death of past sins and a new life in Jesus. This method of baptism is known as immersion.

At the end of the ceremony, some Churches hand a small lighted candle to the baby's parents. This signifies that the baby now belongs to Jesus, the light of the world.

Other denominations like the Baptist and Pentecostal Churches do not believe in baptizing babies. Babies are usually welcomed into the church with a special service of Infant Dedication. Baptism is delayed until the child grows up and requests it. This is known as a **believer's baptism**. It is seen as a very powerful act of personal witness to their faith in Jesus. Personal witness is when someone provides evidence of their faith. Churches which practise believer's baptism think that you must make a personal choice to follow Jesus when you are old enough to understand what the commitment involves. This often happens when people are teenagers, but the age of believers' baptisms can vary. During the service, they publicly take vows and commit themselves to the Christian faith. Believers are also symbolically immersed in water which illustrates their belief in spiritual cleansing, the idea of washing away sin.

Believers' baptisms are usually held in a church building which contains a **baptistry**. A baptistry is a small pool which contains enough water for believers to be fully immersed. Believers' baptism can also take place in the sea or in a river or swimming pool. The River Jordan in Israel, where Jesus is believed to have been baptized, is a popular place for believers' baptisms.

Baptism in the Church of England

The following text, taken from the Church of England's website, describes something of what baptism means for Anglicans.

'Baptism marks the beginning of a journey with God which continues for the rest of our lives… For all involved, particularly the candidates but also parents, godparents and sponsors, it is a joyful moment when we rejoice in what God has done for us in Christ, making serious promises and declaring the faith. The wider community of the local church and friends welcome the new Christian, promising support and prayer for the future…

'The service paints many vivid pictures of what happens on the Christian way. There is the sign of the cross, the badge of faith in the Christian journey, which reminds us of Christ's death for us. Our "drowning" in the water of baptism, where we believe we die to sin and are raised to new life, unites us to Christ's dying and rising… Water is also a sign of new life, as we are born again by water and the Spirit, as Jesus was at his baptism. And as a sign of that new life, there may be a lighted candle, a picture of the light of Christ conquering the darkness of evil. Everyone who is baptized walks in that light for the rest of their lives.'

Confirmation

In this section you will:

- learn about a Christian **rite of passage** called confirmation
- find out why confirmation is important to Christians and what happens during a confirmation service
- gain an understanding of some of the ways in which Christians prepare for confirmation in the Orthodox Church.

Confirmation is important to some **Christians** because it is the service by which they become full adult members of the Christian Church. Confirmation is when they publicly confirm the vows made on their behalf during **infant**

baptism and make their own commitment to the Christian way of life. Many Christians believe that confirmation brings them closer to God and improves their relationship with the Church. They also think it enables people to receive strength and guidance from the Holy Spirit. For some Christians, confirmation means that they can accept Holy Communion (bread and wine) during the Eucharist.

What happens during confirmation?

There is no set age for confirmation. Roman Catholics are usually confirmed when they are about eight years old. Traditionally, in the Church of England, adolescence has been a popular time for confirmation. People preparing for confirmation normally attend confirmation

Young Roman Catholics taking their first Holy Communion

The laying on of hands during confirmation is a symbol of blessing

classes run by their local church. This helps them to understand the teachings of the Christian Church and what is expected of them.

Confirmation services are usually conducted by a bishop. During the ceremony, the person being confirmed is asked a series of questions about their beliefs such as, 'Do you believe and trust in God?' Another important feature of the service is when the bishop places his hands on the head of the candidate and prays. The bishop prays that the **Holy Spirit** will strengthen and guide the person being confirmed. In some Churches, the bishop will also put oil on the candidate's forehead. This symbolizes the gifts or blessings that the Holy Spirit will bring.

In Orthodox Churches there is no separate service of confirmation. Confirmation is carried out by a priest straight after baptism. This service is called **chrismation**. Chrismation involves the baby being anointed or smeared with oil on the forehead, eyes, lips, mouth, nostrils, chest, hands and feet. This symbolizes that the Holy Spirit must energize the whole person in **Christ**. The baby is also given their first **Holy Communion** (bread and wine) on the same occasion.

Denominations which perform **believers' baptism** do not have a confirmation ceremony. Like confirmation, the baptism service is the rite by which they become full adult or grown up members of the Christian Church. It enables them to participate fully in religious practices of their denomination.

What do Christians say about confirmation?

'I decided to get confirmed when I was thirteen. It was the first really big decision that I had made about my life. I got confirmed because I wanted to make a personal commitment to the faith into which I was born. I wanted God to know that I was choosing to be a Christian and not just following the tradition of my parents.'

'I enjoyed going to church but I always felt that something was missing because I could never take bread and wine during the Eucharist. After I got confirmed, I really felt part of the community'.

'My confirmation ceremony was a very moving experience. When the bishop put his hands on my head I felt honoured and humble. I prayed that I would be a good Christian.'

Catechumens

Traditionally, in the Orthodox **Church**, candidates who are preparing or training for baptism are called catechumens. This was a term used by the early church to describe someone who had not yet been initiated into the 'sacred mysteries' of Christianity, but who was undergoing a course of training for that purpose. In the past, all those who were not baptized had to leave the Eucharist service before the bread and wine were brought to the altar.

The Divine **Liturgy** still contains the words: 'All catechumens, depart. Depart, catechumens. All that are catechumens depart. Let no catechumen remain.' Nowadays, however, Orthodox Christians do not actually expect anyone to leave. They keep the phrase to remind them of their responsibility as Christians to share their faith with others who do not believe.

Marriage and funerals

In this section you will:

- learn why marriage is important to Christians
- find out what happens during a Christian marriage ceremony and Christian funeral ceremony
- read about the last rites in the Roman Catholic Church and how they prepare people for death.

Marriage

Christians believe that **marriage** is important because it is a gift or blessing from God. They say that in marriage God brings two people together to love, help and support each other throughout life. The love the couple have for each other is said to reflect the love Jesus had for his followers. Christians believe that through marriage they learn more about God's love for human beings. Christians see marriage as the right relationship for having sexual intercourse and children.

In preparation for their wedding, many couples attend marriage courses run by their church. This helps them to understand the Christian teaching on marriage and the importance of the commitment they are going to make to each other.

What happens during a Christian marriage ceremony?

Each **denomination** has its own marriage ceremony but some features are common to most services. The ceremony usually begins with a hymn which helps people to focus on God. This is followed by a statement which summarizes the purpose of a Christian marriage.

The couple and their guests are then asked if there is any reason they cannot get married. Once the **priest** is satisfied that there are no objections to the marriage, the couple make promises or vows to each other and exchange rings to symbolize their commitment. This is one of the most important parts of the service. Christians believe that they are making their vows before God. The rings, traditionally perfect circles without a beginning or end, symbolize that the promises they have made cannot be broken. Finally, the couple are pronounced husband and wife and prayers are said for them. At the end of the ceremony the newly married couple sign a register to record that the marriage is legal.

In Orthodox churches, after making their vows and exchanging rings, the couple have crowns or garlands placed upon their heads. This symbolizes that the couple have been blessed by God. They also drink wine from the same cup which represents their new life together. Another feature is that the priest leads the couple in a circular procession around the church. This symbolizes that the marriage will have no end.

The bride and groom kneel while the priest blesses them

Death

What happens during a Christian funeral?

Christians believe that there is life after death. This idea is called **eternal life**.

A Christian funeral marks the passing of a believer from this life to eternal life. It also gives people the opportunity to express their feelings and beliefs about death and say goodbye to someone they have cared about. Traditionally, mourners wear dark clothing which symbolizes their sadness. Funeral services take place in a church or **crematorium** chapel. The service usually consists of prayers, hymns, readings and a **sermon** about death, **resurrection** and the life of the person who has died. The ceremony reminds Christians that life is a precious gift from God. They also think about Jesus' death and resurrection. Their belief that Jesus came back to life after he had died brings them comfort and gives them hope for the future. It makes them think that they will meet Jesus and be reunited with their loved ones in Heaven one day. After the funeral service, the body is cremated or buried in a consecrated graveyard. This final part of the ceremony is called the committal.

Last rites

Anglican, Orthodox and Roman Catholic Churches have a series of rituals which can be performed on a dying person. These rituals are often referred to as 'last rites'.

In the Roman Catholic Church, the anointing of the sick, the last **confession** and the receiving of the viaticum are the last rituals or rites of the church.

In the anointing of the sick, the dying person is **anointed** with oil on the eyes, ears, nostrils, mouth and hands. Other parts of the body such as the feet may also be anointed. In the last confession, the dying person confesses their sins to a priest who gives them absolution (forgiveness). The viaticum is the Eucharist or Holy Communion (bread and wine) which is given to a person who is dying. Christians believe that the viaticum provides a dying person with 'spiritual food' which they need for their journey through death to eternal life.

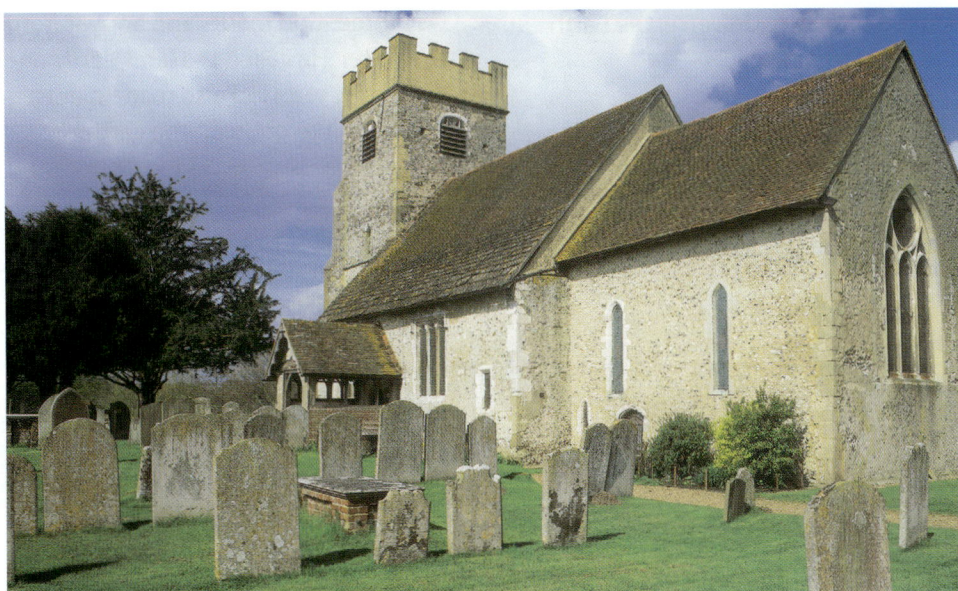

One way Christians remember their loved ones who have died is by dedicating a headstone to them

Creation

In this section you will:

- look at Christian beliefs about creation
- learn how Christians believe the universe came into existence
- gain an understanding of Darwin's theory of evolution.

What do Christians believe about Creation?

Christians believe that God created the universe out of nothing. They say that the wonders and beauty of nature, the complicated way life on earth is arranged and the workings of the solar system means that creation could not have happened by accident. The creation story in Genesis, the first book of the **Old Testament** in the Christian Bible, explains what many Christians believe happened.

The Creation story

When God first created the Universe, the Earth was dark and covered in water.

Day one: God made light and separated it from the darkness. He called the light 'day' and the darkness 'night'.

Day two: God made the sky. He used the sky to divide the water that covered the Earth into two halves.

Day three: God made land appear from beneath the water. He called the land 'earth' and the water the 'sea'. God also made plants, trees and vegetation to grow on the earth.

Day four: God made the sun, moon and stars to light up the sky and separate night from day.

Day five: God made all the creatures that live on the earth. He made fish for the sea, birds for the air and animals and insects for the land.

Day six: God made human beings. He put them in charge of everything he had created and told them to look after it.

Day seven: God rested. The universe was complete.

What is the Christian attitude towards the Creation story?

Christians have different attitudes towards the Creation story. Some fundamentalist Christians believe that the Creation story is an accurate account of what literally happened. Most Christians, however, think that the Creation story is a myth. Myths are stories that explain mysterious events, unusual traditions or extraordinary sights in nature. They are usually ancient and have been passed on by word of mouth for hundreds of years before being written down. Many people think myths contain some truth without being accurate historical accounts or scientific explanations of what they describe.

Some scientists have criticized Christian beliefs about creation. They and others believe in the theory of **evolution**. They say that science has proved that it took much longer than six days for the universe to be formed. Many Christians agree with this. They believe that the word 'day', in the Creation story, is a metaphor for a much longer period of time.

Astronomers have also criticized Christian ideas about creation. They believe that a massive explosion in space about eighteen billion years ago was responsible for the formation of the universe. This is called the Big Bang theory. Christians say that this theory supports their belief that God created the universe out of nothing.

Darwin's theory of evolution

Charles Darwin (1809–1882 CE) was a clergyman in the **Church** of England. He worked for five years as an unpaid naturalist on the HMS *Beagle* scientific mission, on the Pacific Coast of South America. The research he did on this voyage helped him to develop a theory of evolution which accounted for the origins and diversity of life on Earth. Darwin set out his ideas in a controversial book called *The Origins of Species*.

According to Darwin, human beings evolved from a primitive species and were not a unique creation of God. His ideas challenged Christian beliefs about creation, and caused people to question the accuracy and reliability of the biblical accounts.

The environment

Why do Christians believe they should care for the environment?

Christians believe that the Earth and everything in it belongs to God. They believe that God appointed human beings to be stewards or managers of the Earth and look after it. The idea that human beings have a responsibility to look after the Earth is known as **stewardship**. Christians also believe that human beings will eventually have to account to God for the way in which they have treated Creation.

Another reason Christians look after the environment is that they realize that they are dependent upon it for things that they need to live such as food, water and oxygen. They are reminded of their dependence upon Creation during weekly worship and at other times during the year. In the autumn Christians have a Harvest Festival. Traditionally, this is a time of celebration, thanksgiving and praise for 'the harvest of the fields' such as fruits, vegetables and grains. Nowadays displays of various foods are made in church and services are held to praise God and thank Him for His goodness.

The food is usually distributed afterwards to the elderly and those in need.

How do Christians care for the environment?

Christians fulfil their responsibility to look after the Earth in a variety of ways. Some of the things they might do include disposing of litter properly, recycling rubbish and only buying products which are packaged using biodegradable materials. They have also set up several Christian organizations which work to protect the environment on a larger scale.

The Christian Ecology Link (CEL) encourages Christians throughout Britain to think seriously about environmental issues. It helps them to understand their responsibilities towards the environment and suggests ways that they can help to protect it. The CEL publishes a magazine called *Green Christians* which informs people about their work. It also organizes events such as a National Car-free Day, a Festival of Cycling and Walk to School Weeks which are designed to focus the public's attention on the damage cars can do to people's health and the environment.

Another organization, the European Christian Environmental Network (ECEN), encourages Christians in 26 countries throughout Europe to get involved in a wide range of environmental work. Some of the issues they deal with include climate change and genetic engineering.

Christian Ecology Link (CEL) symbol

European Christian Environmental Network (ECEN) symbol

Christian aid agencies try to set up self-sustainable programmes of development. Here, CAFOD are distributing buckets in Albania

Christian Aid agencies such as CAFOD, Christian Aid and Tearfund have a role to play too. They show how environmental abuse can affect the quality of people's lives. These organizations work in some of the poorest countries of the world and campaign for a more caring and just distribution of the Earth's resources.

CAFOD

There are a number of Christian charities which aim to care for the Earth and those who live on it. CAFOD, the Catholic Agency for Overseas Development, is a British charity which works to eradicate poverty in the world's poorest countries. The charity believes that the world's resources are a gift from God and should be shared equally between all human beings. It provides education, skills training, healthcare, safe water, and agricultural and small business development programmes for communities in developing countries.

Christian Aid and Tearfund

Christian Aid aims to put an end to poverty and works to change the international trade laws which keep the world's poorest people poor. One issue of concern is child labour. There are thought to be about 250 million working children throughout the world, many of whom are denied an education and a proper childhood.

Tearfund is an evangelical Christian development charity. One of its projects is Tearcraft, which sells a range of fairly traded products throughout the United Kingdom and Ireland.

Moral issues 1

In this section you will:
- learn how Christians decide what is right and wrong
- find out about the Christian attitude to animal rights
- read and think about the story of Noah in the Christian Old Testament.

What is a moral issue?

Morality is about right and wrong behaviour. A **moral** issue is a situation which might be considered to be right or wrong for a variety of reasons, such as the laws of a country, the teachings of a religion or the beliefs and values of an individual or community. A moral decision is where a choice has to be made between what is the right thing to do and the wrong thing to do. Not all the decisions people have to make are moral decisions.

The word **immoral** means 'wrong'. An immoral act is an action that is thought to be morally wrong. This means that it is an unacceptable way to behave.

The word **amoral** means 'without moral standards or principles'. Someone who is amoral shows no understanding of what is right or wrong.

How do Christians decide what is right and wrong?

Christians try to live their lives in the way they think God wants. They believe that God sent Jesus to show them the right way to live. When making a moral decision, many Christians would ask 'what would Jesus do in this situation?' and try to follow his example. Jesus' life and teachings are the main source of moral authority for most Christians. A source of authority is something or someone which tells a person what to do.

Christians can find out what Jesus might have done by reading the **Gospels** in the Bible. The Bible also contains laws and other information about the right way to live such as the Ten Commandments and the words of the **prophets**. Using the Bible as a source of authority can sometimes be difficult for Christians. This is because the world in which the writers of the Bible and Jesus lived was very different to the world today. The issues modern Christians have to face may not be mentioned specifically in the Bible. In some situations, the Bible can only act as a guide and Christians must think things through carefully themselves and follow their own conscience. Christians might also look at what the official teachings of their Church say about an issue and ask the advice of other Christians.

Animal rights

Christians believe that animals are an important part of God's creation but they have different views about how animals should be treated. Most Christians think that animals do not have the same rights as human beings but they should still be treated with kindness and respect. Many Christians disagree with 'blood sports', intensive farming methods and using animals for toiletries and cosmetic testing. Some Christians, however, accept that using animals to test the safety of medicines and chemicals and to improve veterinary knowledge can be helpful.

Wolves and sheep will live together in peace
and leopards will lie down with young goats.
Calves and lion cubs will feed together,
and little children will take care of them.
Cows and bears will eat together,
and their calves and cubs will lie down in peace.
Lions will eat straw as cattle do.
Even a baby will not be harmed
if it plays near a poisonous snake.

Isaiah 11: 6–8

The ACC encourages Christians and non-Christians to get involved in animal welfare issues. Another part of their work includes organizing church services where worshippers pray for suffering animals. Some churches allow pets to attend these services This idea is based on a verse in the Bible, Ephesians 1: 10, which says that all of creation should come together to worship God.

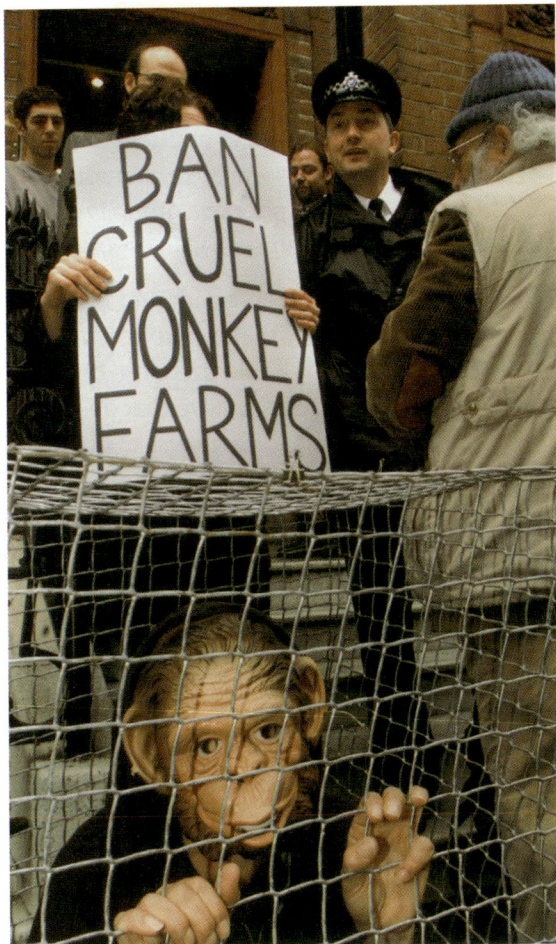

An animal rights protest against Spanish monkey farms

Other Christians say that human beings should live in harmony with animals and not exploit them in any way whatsoever. The Religious Society of Friends, Quakers, have always been very concerned about the rights of animals. A large number of Christians who belong to this denomination are vegetarians. Most Quakers would also disagree with fur coats, circuses which use animals and zoos.

Christians founded the RSPCA and there are other Christian organizations which work to protect the rights of animals. A lady called May Tripp set up the Animal Christian Concern (ACC) society. She noticed that her dog had his own unique personality and needs. One day when he was in pain May thought about how animals being hunted or experimented on suffered and she decided to do something to protect them.

The story of Noah

God said to Noah, 'I have decided to put an end to the whole human race. I will destroy them completely, because the world is full of their violent deeds. Build a boat for yourself out of good timber; make rooms in it and cover it with tar inside and out. Make it 133 metres long, 22 metres wide, and 13 metres high. Make a roof for the boat and leave a space of 44 centimetres between the roof and the sides. Build it with three decks and put a door in the side. I am going to send a flood on the earth to destroy every living being. Everything on the earth will die, but I will make a covenant with you. Go into the boat with your wife, your sons, and their wives. Take into the boat with you a male and a female of every kind of animal and of every kind of bird, in order to keep them alive. Take along all kinds of food for you and for them.' Noah did everything that God commanded.

(Genesis 6: 13–22)

'Every kind of animal and bird… went onto the boat with Noah, as God has commanded.' (Genesis 7: 8, 9)

Moral issues 2

In this section you will:

In this section you will:
- find how Christians believe people should treat each other
- learn about the Christian attitude towards prejudice and discrimination
- read about people who work for equality and justice.

Prejudice is when you prejudge someone. This means that you form an opinion about them without knowing what they are like.
Discrimination is when you act on your prejudice and treat some people better or worse than other people because of what you believe to be true about them. There are many different kinds of prejudice and people can be discriminated against for a variety of reasons such as size, accent, colour of skin, gender, age, ability and race. Discrimination on the basis of race or colour of skin is known as racism. Treating people the same way regardless of their status, physical characteristics or mental abilities is called equality.

Prejudice can lead to stereotyping. This is when you form fixed mental images about what a particular group of people are like. Stereotyping assumes that every member of a group is the same and will act the same way.

Christian teachings disagree with prejudice and discrimination. They say that everyone is created and loved by God and should therefore be treated equally. Christians believe that one of the reasons Jesus came to Earth was to put an end to prejudice and discrimination.

According to the Bible, Jesus did not discriminate against anyone. He told his followers that they must treat other people as they would like to be treated themselves. This is known as the Golden Rule. Jesus taught that part of loving God included loving their neighbour as themselves. Using the **parable** of the Good Samaritan, found in Luke 10: 25–37 in the **New Testament**, Jesus explained that the term 'neighbour' meant everyone, particularly people in need. The kind of love Christians must try and show to others is called **agape**.

Agape is an unconditional and self-sacrificing love. It involves putting yourself out to help others and expecting nothing in return.

'…God treats everyone on the same basis.'

(Acts 10: 24)

'…From one human being [God] created all races on earth and made them live, throughout the whole earth.'

(Acts 17: 26)

'…there is no difference between Jews and Gentiles, between slaves and free men, between men and women; you are all one in union with Christ Jesus.'

(Galatians 3: 28)

How have Christians responded to prejudice and discrimination?

Dr Martin Luther King

Dr Martin Luther King, a black American civil rights leader, fought for the equal treatment of black and white people in the Southern States of America, using non-violent forms of protest. He was assassinated in 1968.

'…I have a dream that my four little children will one day live in a nation where they will not be judged by the colour of their skin but by the content of their character…'

Dr Martin Luther King

Nelson Mandela

Nelson Mandela, a black South African leader, was imprisoned for 28 years for his opposition to **apartheid**, a system of racial segregation in South Africa. He was released from prison in 1990 and continues to work for the equal treatment of black people in South Africa.

'…Let there be justice for all. Let there be peace for all. Let there be work, bread, water and salt for all…'

Nelson Mandela

Mother Teresa

Many Christians believe that Mother Teresa is a good example of agape love

Mother Teresa, a Roman Catholic nun, devoted her life to caring for the 'poorest of the poor' in India. She fought against poverty and disease and helped people regardless of their race or religion.

'There is only one God and He is God to all; therefore it is important that everyone is seen as equal before God.'
I've always said we should help a Hindu become a better Hindu, a Muslim become a better Muslim, a Catholic become a better Catholic.'

Mother Teresa

Churches' Commission for Racial Justice

The Churches' Commission for Racial Justice (CCRJ) is an **ecumenical** organization which monitors racial justice in Britain, Ireland and Europe. It also organizes and coordinates the **Churches'** response to important issues or developments.

The CCRJ helps Churches to provide educational programmes about racial justice. Some of the main areas of work include providing support for victims of racial attacks and the Free Families From Fear Campaign.

The second Sunday in September is Racial Justice Sunday. This is an opportunity for all Christians in Britain and Ireland to join together and **pray** for racial justice.

Logo of the CCRJ

In this section you will:

● explore some Christian responses to ultimate questions

● have the opportunity to think about how the existence of God could help to explain some of life's mysteries

● read and reflect upon a Christian poem about death.

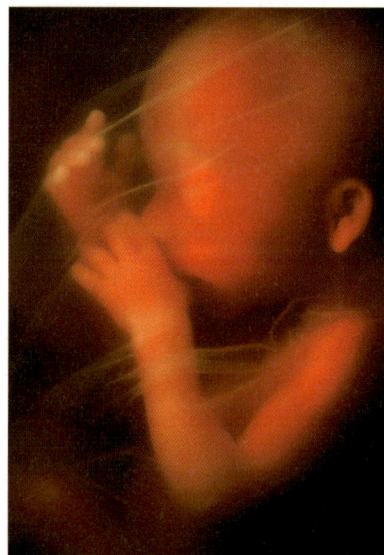

What is an ultimate question?

Ultimate questions are very important questions to which there are no definite or absolute answers, like 'Does God exist?' or 'How did everything begin?' They are usually questions about something in life which is difficult to understand, explain or prove. People often ask ultimate questions to try and make sense of the world in which they live. They also ask ultimate questions to find purpose and meaning in their lives. There are many things in life that cannot easily be explained and the way people respond to or answer ultimate questions depends on their beliefs. Many people believe that the existence of God can explain these mysteries. Christianity, like other religions, has beliefs which try to provide answers to ultimate questions or give people hope that there may be answers to them.

Why do we exist?

'Then God said, "And now we will make human beings; they will be like us and resemble us…" So God created human beings, making them to be like himself. He created them male and female…'

Genesis 1: 26–7

Christians believe that all life is a precious gift from God. They say that we exist because God has chosen to give us life. Christians believe that every individual is unique and special because they are created, known and loved by God. The idea that all life is sacred because it comes from God is called the **sanctity of life** . The Christian belief in the sanctity of life affects how they deal with issues such as genetic engineering, embryo technology, abortion and euthanasia.

What are we here for?

'My commandment is this: love one another as I have loved you.' (John 15: 12)

Christians believe that God created human beings for a reason. They say that life on earth is part of God's plan for human beings. Christians believe that human beings were made to have a personal relationship with God which begins in this life and continues after death. They claim that life on Earth gives human beings the opportunity to get to know God and develop their relationship with Him. Christians say that their purpose in life is to love and serve God. This involves helping and caring for other people, as Christians believe that all human beings are made in the 'image' of God. They take this to mean that people have godlike characteristics and should therefore be valued and respected, not that they are exactly like God.

'The dying, the cripple, the mental, the unwanted, the unloved – they are all Jesus in disguise.'

Mother Teresa

What happens when we die?

Christians believe that life is eternal. This means that it continues after death. Christians think that the soul, a person's spirit, lives on after death.

They believe that human beings are given life by God in the beginning and have the opportunity to be with God when they die. Christians claim that what happens to us after death depends on how we have lived our lives on Earth. If we have led a good life we will be in the presence of God and experience a state known as Heaven. If we have led a bad life we will be apart from God and experience a state known as Hell. Some Christians argue that not many people can hope to enter Heaven straight away. Roman Catholics believe that most people go through another stage of preparation called '**purgatory**'.

It is not death to die

This poem illustrates the positive way in which Christians face death.

It is not death to die,
To leave this weary road,
And, 'midst the brotherhood on high,
To be at home with God.

It is not death to close
The eye long dimm'd by tears,
And wake in glorious repose
To spend eternal years.

It is not death to fling
Aside this sinful dust,
And rise, on strong exulting wing,
To live among the just.

Jesus, Thou Prince of life!
Thy chosen cannot die;
Like Thee, they conquer in the strife,
To reign with Thee on high.

George W. Bethune, 1847

For me to live is Christ, and to die is gain.
(Philippians 1: 21)

In this section you will:

● look at how Christians respond to the problems of evil and suffering

● have the opportunity to reflect upon some of the issues raised such as the existence of God and the origins of evil.

Flooding in the United Kingdom

Why do people suffer?

One of the most difficult questions to answer is 'why do people suffer?' It is a particularly difficult question to answer if, like **Christians**, you believe in an all-loving, all-powerful and all-knowing God. Many people argue that there is so much suffering in the world that God cannot possibly exist. They say that if God did exist He or She would not allow human beings to suffer. Other people say that even if God does exist the large amount of suffering in the world means that God's powers are limited in some way. Some people also say that suffering is a fact of life. It is part of what it means to be human and without God's help and support life would sometimes be unbearable.

People's ideas and beliefs about suffering can also change according to their experiences. For religious people, personal suffering is often a test of faith. Some lose their faith and turn away from God whilst others claim that the difficult experiences in their lives have made them better people, strengthened their faith and brought them closer to God. There are also people who have become religious as a result of their suffering.

'My faith died along with my daughter. I gave her a Christian burial because everyone expected that of me but as I stood at her graveside I thought this is pointless. There is no God.'

'I was christened as a baby but I never really thought about God at all until I became ill with cancer. One day when I was feeling depressed and unhappy, a friend of mine, who is a Christian, persuaded me to go to church with her. I came out of the service feeling a sense of peace and I felt hopeful about my life. I went to church regularly after that and I've recently decided to get confirmed.'

Where does suffering come from?

There are many different causes of suffering. Sometimes suffering occurs as a result of a natural disaster such as an earthquake or flooding. It is described as natural because it does not seem to result from human action.

The devastation caused by an earthquake in India

Suffering can also be caused by human beings through deliberate acts of violence such as murder, terrorism and war. This kind of suffering is the result of human-made or moral evil. The word 'evil' means 'wrong or wicked'. We say something is evil when it causes harm or injury to people.

Not all causes of suffering fit into these two categories. For example, human beings sometimes cause suffering to others accidentally and some natural disasters are the result of humans misusing or abusing natural resources.

What is the Christian response to suffering?

The Christian writer C. S. Lewis (author of the *Chronicles of Narnia*) once said that 'pain was God's megaphone for rousing a deaf world'. He thought that pain and suffering was God's way of getting people to turn to him. C. S. Lewis also likened God to a sculptor trying to create a perfect statue. He said that pain and suffering was God's chisel, His way of making us become better people.

Christians have different ideas and beliefs about why people suffer and what the presence of suffering in the world means. Most Christians believe that the majority of suffering in the world is caused by human sin. They believe that when God created human beings he gave them **free will**. This means that they are able to choose how to behave. When human beings turn away from God and do evil things it results in suffering. Some Christians believe that there is a supernatural evil force called the Devil (Satan) which encourages human beings to do wicked things. They believe that the Devil is responsible for all the evil in the world.

Other Christians see suffering as kind of test. They get this idea from a book in the Bible called Job which tells the story of a man who is tested by suffering to see if he will continue to worship, praise and believe in God. Another view is that you shouldn't question God about suffering.

You just have to trust that God knows what He or She is doing. There is also the idea that you will be rewarded after death for the suffering you experience on Earth.

Most Christians believe that God understands suffering and pain. They say that by becoming a man in Jesus God knows what it is like to suffer. Christians are taught that they should keep worshipping, praising and believing in God no matter what happens.

Euthanasia

The word euthanasia means 'easy death'. It refers to the early ending of a person's life to prevent them from unnecessary pain and suffering. Euthanasia is a very controversial issue and people have different views about it. At the moment, euthanasia is illegal in almost every country. Many people, however, think that the laws should be changed. They say that a person suffering from an incurable illness should be allowed the option of a painless and early death if that is what they want.

All the Christian **Churches** are against euthanasia. They say that God gives life to human beings and only God can end it. The Christian alternative to euthanasia is a hospice. A hospice is a place which looks after people who are terminally ill. Hospices aim to relieve pain through medication, and to provide support and counselling to the person who is dying and their families. The first hospices were founded by Christians.

Glossary

Agape unconditional, self-sacrificing, non-romantic love which Christians believe they should try and demonstrate to others

Amoral without moral qualities, characteristics

Anointed being smeared with consecrated oil

Anointing of the Sick being anointed with holy oil during some ceremonies

Apartheid a system of racial segregation in South Africa

Apocrypha (from a Greek word meaning 'hidden') a collection of seven books which the Roman Catholic Church accepts as part of its scriptures

Apostles (from the Greek word 'to send') the name given to the original twelve disciples of Jesus. Christians believe they were 'sent out' into the world by God to tell people about Jesus

Apparition the appearance of a supernatural figure

Ascension the belief that Jesus went up (ascended) into the presence of God (Heaven)

Atonement the idea of being 'at one' or reconciled with God through the death of Jesus

Baptism the ceremony by which some people become members of the Christian Church

Baptistry a small pool containing enough water for a person to be fully immersed during a baptism ceremony

Believers' baptism a ceremony by which young people or adults become full members of the Christian Church

Blasphemy being disrespectful to God

Chrismation a ceremony carried out straight after baptism in the Orthodox Church

Christ the name given to Jesus by his followers after his death when they believed he had been resurrected

Christians the name given to the followers of the Christ (Jesus)

Church the name given to the building in which Christians worship; different denominations within Christianity; the worldwide Christian community

Clergy a group of people who are ordained and authorized to lead worship and look after the congregation of a church in a Christian denomination

Confession the act of admitting to God, through a priest, what one has done wrong and expressing sorrow and regret for it

Confirmation the ceremony where Christians publicly confirm the vows made on their behalf at baptism and become full or grown up members of the Christian Church

Congregation a group of people who have gathered together for worship

Consecrated holy, blessed, set apart; something which is made holy and set aside for religious purposes

Creed (from the Latin word *credo* meaning 'I believe') a statement of belief

Crematorium a building in which corpses are cremated

Cross the symbol of Christianity

Crucifix a particular kind of cross which has an image of Jesus on it

Denomination a separate Christian group which shares the same name and beliefs

Disciples followers of Jesus including the twelve men Jesus chose especially to help him carry out his work on earth

Discrimination the action taken as a result of prejudice

Divine godlike

Easter Day the day Christians celebrate their belief in Jesus' resurrection, one of the most joyful and happy days in the Christian year

Ecumenical belonging to the 'world-wide' Christian Church

Episcopal (from the Greek word meaning 'bishop') a term used to describe a Church which has bishops

Epistles long and usually quite formal letters containing Christian teachings

Eternal life the belief that life continues after death

Eucharist the name given to a service of Holy Communion; it means 'thanksgiving'

Evolution the gradual and natural development of the universe over a long period of time

Forgiveness to forgive or be forgiven, to stop thinking badly of someone or no longer be thought of badly because of wrongdoings

Free will the idea that God has given human beings the freedom to choose how to behave

Genuflection a series of movements made during worship which show respect for God

Good Friday the day on which Christians remember Jesus' death

Gospels (from a Greek word meaning 'good news') the first four books of the New Testament: Matthew, Mark, Luke and John. These tell the story of Jesus and his teachings.

Great Schism the split of the Christian Church into two parts, the Catholic Church and the Orthodox Church, in 1054

Hebrew the language of the Jewish people

Heresy a belief which is different to the official teachings of the Christian Church

Holy associated with God, sacred

Holy Communion a church service during which Christians share bread and wine together in memory of Jesus; the act of receiving bread and wine during the Eucharist

Holy Saturday the last day of Lent, the day before Easter Day, when Christians get ready to celebrate their belief in Jesus' resurrection

Holy Spirit the third person of the Trinity, an invisible divine power which guides and inspires human beings

Holy water water which has been blessed and put aside for holy purposes such as baptism

Holy Week the period in the Christian year when Christians focus on the events associated with the death and resurrection of Jesus

Humility being humble, showing that you recognize your failings and weaknesses

Immoral unacceptable, wrong behaviour

Incarnation the act of God becoming a human being in Jesus

Incense a sweet smelling substance which gives off an odour when burnt

Infant baptism a ceremony by which children are welcomed into the Christian Church

Interfaith involving different religions

Laity ordinary members of a Christian congregation who have not been ordained

Last Supper the name given to the final meal Jesus shared with his disciples

Lectionary a book containing an ordered set of Bible readings for Christians to study at set times throughout the year

Liturgy (from a Greek word meaning 'service') set form of service used by a church

Marriage the religious or legal ceremony by which people become 'man and wife'

Martyrs people who suffer or die for their beliefs

Maundy Thursday the day before Good Friday when Christians remember the final meal or Last Supper Jesus had with his disciples

Meditation a form of quiet prayer which involves clearing the mind of all distractions and concentrating on God

Messiah (Mashiah) Hebrew word meaning the 'Anointed One', a saviour sent from God

Midnight Mass special service held late at night on Christmas Eve to commemorate the birth of Jesus

Ministry time spent in the service of God

Missionaries people who are sent to places by their church to spread the Christian faith.

Moral conforming to accepted good standards of general behaviour

New Testament a collection of Christian writings which include the Gospels

Old Testament the Christian name for the Jewish scriptures, the first part of the Christian Bible

Ordination the service by which a person becomes a priest

Pacifists people who disagree with the use of violence

Pagan an ancient religion based on the natural world

Palm Sunday the day Christians commemorate Jesus arriving in Jerusalem on a donkey shortly before he was crucified. It is the last Sunday of Lent and the first day of Holy Week

Parable a short story which makes a religious or moral point

Paschal candle a large candle which is lit in many churches on Holy Saturday to represent the light of Jesus

Penance a voluntary act to make up or atone for wrongdoings

Pesach (Passover) Jewish festival which reminds the Jews of how God rescued them from slavery in Egypt

Pilgrim the name given to someone who goes on a religious journey or pilgrimage

Pilgrimage a religious journey

Pope the leader of the Roman Catholic Church

Prayer a way of approaching or communicating with God

Prejudice to prejudge someone for no good reason

Priest the title given to people who have been ordained and are authorized to lead worship and look after the congregation in the Anglican, Roman Catholic and Orthodox Churches. Priests are also known as vicars in the Church of England

Prophets important people in the Bible who are believed to have been inspired by God

Protestant (from the word 'protest') the name given to the new Churches which were formed as a result of the Reformation

Psalms a collection of 150 religious songs, poems and prayers which are sung or chanted during Christian services or ceremonies

Purgatory according to Roman Catholic belief, a state after death where the soul is purified and made ready to go to Heaven

Reconciliation the idea that Jesus' death repaired the relationship between God and human beings and brought them together

Redeemer a title Christians have given to Jesus because they believe he rescued or freed people from the consequences of their sins

Redemption the idea of Jesus saving human beings from the consequences of their sins

Reformation a religious revolution in the Catholic Church during the sixteenth century

Repentance showing regret for wrongdoings, turning away from sin and living the way God wants

Resurrection the belief that Jesus rose from the dead and overcame death

Revelation God revealing or making Himself/Herself known to human beings

Rites of passage rituals which mark important human experiences such as baptism, confirmation, marriage and death

Sacrament a sacred experience or event where Christians believe they receive special blessings from God

Saint someone who has been recognized after their death as being especially holy and dedicated to God whilst they were alive

Salvation being saved from sin, having a personal relationship with God

Salvation Army a Protestant denomination founded by William Booth in 1865, which is organized in a military way and has its own uniform

Sanctity of life the idea that all life is precious and sacred because it is a gift from God

Saviour a person who has saved someone. This is a title Christians have given Jesus because they believe he saved people from the consequences of their sins

Scriptures writings inspired by God

Second Coming the belief that Jesus will return to Earth one day to finally judge human beings

Secular non-religious

Sermon the part of the service when the priest talks to the congregation about some aspect of Christian belief and practice

Shrine a special area associated with a holy person or object

Sins thoughts or actions that go against the will of God

Stewardship the idea that human beings have a responsibility to look after the earth

Tenakh Jewish name for the Old Testament

Transubstantiation the belief that the bread and wine actually became the body and blood of Jesus Christ during the Eucharist

Trinity the belief that there are three persons within the one God: God the Father, God the Son and God the Holy Spirit

Vestments special clothing worn by members of the clergy when they take part in worship

Virgin Mary a title given to Mary the mother of Jesus which reflects the Christian belief that she was a pure and good person

Index